Agent Flow

Design Dynamic AI Workflows with LangChain and LangGraph

James Acklin

Copyright Page

Table of Contents

Preface

The future of artificial intelligence (AI) is not just about creating smarter algorithms—it's about building intelligent systems that can adapt, learn, and work autonomously. As AI continues to advance, the need for dynamic, scalable, and flexible workflows has become more critical than ever. Traditional static systems are no longer sufficient to handle the growing complexity and scale of modern applications. This book, *Agent Flow: Designing Dynamic AI Workflows with LangChain and LangGraph*, aims to bridge this gap by providing a comprehensive guide to building adaptive AI systems using cutting-edge tools.

The frameworks LangChain and LangGraph have revolutionized the way AI workflows are designed and implemented. They enable developers to create intelligent agents capable of managing complex, interconnected tasks with a high degree of flexibility and autonomy. From automating business processes to developing sophisticated conversational AI systems, these tools are unlocking new possibilities in AI development.

This book was born from a recognition of the growing demand for dynamic AI systems that are scalable, secure, and adaptable. Developers and organizations are seeking solutions that can handle the increasing complexity of data, real-time decision-making, and seamless integration with emerging technologies. Whether it's orchestrating multiple agents, integrating external APIs, or managing workflows at scale, LangChain and LangGraph offer the tools necessary to meet these challenges head-on.

Purpose of This Book

The goal of this book is to provide a practical, hands-on guide to designing and deploying dynamic AI workflows. It combines theoretical insights with real-world applications, guiding readers from foundational concepts to advanced implementations. Throughout this book, you will learn how to:

- Understand the core components of dynamic AI workflows and autonomous agents.
- Set up and configure development environments for LangChain and LangGraph.
- Design adaptive workflows that can respond to real-time data and changing conditions.
- Integrate external APIs, data sources, and specialized tools to extend agent capabilities.
- Deploy scalable AI systems in production environments while ensuring performance, security, and reliability.
- Implement error handling, workflow recovery, and continuous improvement strategies.
- Explore emerging trends and how AI workflows are evolving to meet future demands.

Why This Book Matters

The concepts and tools covered in this book are not just theoretical—they are practical, actionable, and designed to solve real-world problems. As industries across healthcare, finance, manufacturing, and technology continue to adopt AI-driven solutions, the ability to design flexible and intelligent workflows will be a highly valuable skill.

This book emphasizes not only how to build these systems but also how to do so **responsibly** and **ethically**. We explore strategies for ensuring fairness, transparency, and security in AI workflows. Readers will also gain insight into how the open-source community plays a critical role in advancing AI technologies and how they can contribute to this growing ecosystem.

How This Book Is Structured

To guide you through the journey of mastering dynamic AI workflows, this book is organized into well-structured chapters:

- Chapters 1–3 cover foundational knowledge, including AI workflows, LangChain, and LangGraph architectures.
- Chapters 4–6 focus on designing intelligent agents, building adaptive workflows, and optimizing performance.
- Chapters 7–9 provide practical guidance on deployment, scalability, and real-world projects.
- Chapter 10 explores future trends in AI systems and how to stay ahead in this rapidly evolving field.

Each chapter is designed to build upon the previous one, gradually expanding your understanding and capabilities. To reinforce learning, the book includes detailed code examples, practical exercises, and real-world applications.

Who This Book Is For

This book is written for:

- Software Developers and Engineers who want to build dynamic, scalable AI solutions.
- Data Scientists and Machine Learning Practitioners looking to automate workflows and deploy models efficiently.
- AI Researchers and Enthusiasts eager to explore cutting-edge tools for designing intelligent systems.
- Tech Entrepreneurs and Product Managers interested in integrating AI workflows into products and services.
- Students and Educators seeking a practical, hands-on resource for learning AI workflow design.

Whether you're a beginner or an experienced developer, this book will meet you where you are and guide you toward building powerful, adaptable AI systems.

Acknowledgments

This book would not have been possible without the contributions of countless innovators, researchers, and developers in the AI and open-source communities. Special thanks to the teams behind **LangChain** and **LangGraph** for creating such transformative tools and fostering an environment that encourages collaboration and innovation. To the contributors, maintainers, and users who continue to improve these frameworks, your work inspires the future of AI development.

Finally, a heartfelt thank you to the readers. Your curiosity and drive to learn and build better AI systems are what push this field forward. It is my hope that this book empowers you to design AI workflows that make a meaningful impact in your work and the world.

Let's Begin

The future of AI is dynamic, intelligent, and adaptable. Let's build it—one workflow at a time.

James Acklin

Chapter 1: Introduction

1.1 Understanding AI Workflows

At its most basic level, an AI workflow is a sequence of steps that takes raw data as input and produces a meaningful, actionable output. These steps involve data collection, preprocessing, model execution, decision-making, and often integration with external systems. But modern AI workflows go beyond this linear process—they are dynamic, interactive, and adaptable.

Why Are AI Workflows Important?

AI workflows allow systems to automate complex tasks that typically require human intelligence. This automation isn't just about speed; it's about making systems more intelligent, adaptable, and capable of making context-aware decisions. Whether it's a chatbot handling customer inquiries or a financial model analyzing market trends, the backbone of these systems is a well-structured AI workflow.

Key Components of an AI Workflow

1. Data Input: Every workflow starts with data. This could be text from a user query, sensor data from IoT devices, or structured data from databases. The type of data defines how the workflow begins.
2. Preprocessing: Raw data is rarely ready for direct use. Preprocessing involves cleaning, formatting, and transforming the data to make it suitable for the next steps. For text, this could be tokenization; for images, resizing or filtering.
3. Model Execution: This is where machine learning or AI models come into play. The model takes the preprocessed

input and produces predictions, classifications, or recommendations.

4. Decision Logic: The output from the model often isn't the final answer. It might need additional processing or validation. Decision logic determines the next step—whether to generate a response, trigger another process, or involve another model.

5. Action/Integration: The workflow often interacts with external systems, like sending a response to a user, updating a database, or calling another API.

6. Feedback Loop (Optional): In advanced workflows, the system learns from user feedback to improve future decisions. This is critical for systems that adapt over time.

A Simple AI Workflow Example

Let's make this concrete with a simple example: a chatbot that answers frequently asked questions.

1. Input: The user sends a message: *"What are your store hours?"*

2. Preprocessing: The text is cleaned and converted into a format suitable for processing.

3. Model Execution: A natural language understanding (NLU) model detects the user's intent.

4. Decision Logic: Based on the intent, the system decides whether to retrieve store hours from a database or handle it differently.

5. Action: The system fetches store hours and sends the answer back to the user.

6. Feedback: If the user gives a thumbs down, the system logs the feedback for improvement.

This is a **basic AI workflow**. Now, let's write a simple version of this process in Python.

Code Example: Basic Chatbot Workflow with LangChain

```python
from langchain import OpenAI, LLMChain

from langchain.prompts import PromptTemplate


# Step 1: Define a prompt template

prompt = PromptTemplate(

    input_variables=["question"],

    template="Answer the following customer
question: {question}"

)


# Step 2: Initialize the language model

llm_chain = LLMChain(llm=OpenAI(), prompt=prompt)


# Step 3: Simulate user input

user_question = "What are your store hours?"


# Step 4: Run the workflow

response = llm_chain.run(user_question)

print(response)
```

Explanation of the Workflow:

- Step 1: We create a prompt to instruct the model on how to handle customer questions.
- Step 2: We initialize an OpenAI model wrapped in a chain, ready to process the input.
- Step 3: We simulate a customer asking about store hours.
- Step 4: The model processes the input and generates a response.

This example is intentionally simple but captures the flow of data from input to output.

Types of AI Workflows

AI workflows can range from simple linear pipelines to complex, multi-branch systems. Let's discuss some of the most common types.

1. Linear Workflows (Sequential): These are straightforward and step-by-step. Each step feeds into the next.

Example:
A text classification system that:

- Takes text input → Preprocesses it → Runs it through a classifier → Outputs a category.

2. Branching Workflows: These workflows adapt based on conditions. The next step depends on the model's output or external inputs.

Example:
In a customer service chatbot, if the user is asking about billing, the workflow might access a billing database. If it's a technical issue, it routes the query to tech support.

3. Parallel Workflows: Some tasks can be run simultaneously to improve efficiency.

Example:

A content recommendation engine might simultaneously analyze user behavior and trending topics to generate personalized suggestions.

4. Feedback-Driven Workflows (Reinforcement): These workflows learn from interactions and improve over time.

Example:

A recommendation system that adapts based on what content users engage with the most.

Real-World Example: AI in E-commerce

Let's apply these concepts to a real-world scenario: an AI-powered product recommendation system for an online store.

Workflow Breakdown:

1. Input: User visits the website and views a few products.
2. Preprocessing: Collect and analyze browsing behavior (e.g., product categories, time spent on pages).
3. Model Execution: A recommendation model predicts similar or complementary products.
4. Decision Logic: If the user has added items to the cart, prioritize upsell items. If not, suggest trending products.
5. Action: Display recommended products on the page.
6. Feedback Loop: Track clicks and purchases to refine future recommendations.

Code Example: Product Recommendation Workflow

```
import random

# Step 1: Define user behavior data

user_browsing_history = ["wireless headphones",
"Bluetooth speakers", "smartwatch"]
```

```python
# Step 2: Simple recommendation logic

def recommend_products(history):

    recommendations = {

        "wireless headphones": ["Noise-cancelling headphones", "Headphone cases"],

        "Bluetooth speakers": ["Portable speakers", "Smart home speakers"],

        "smartwatch": ["Fitness trackers", "Smartphone accessories"]

    }

    suggested = []

    for item in history:

        suggested.extend(recommendations.get(item, []))

    return random.sample(suggested, 3)   # Return 3 random recommendations


# Step 3: Run the workflow

recommended_items = recommend_products(user_browsing_history)

print("Recommended for you:", recommended_items)
```

Output Example:

Recommended for you: ['Smartphone accessories', 'Noise-cancelling headphones', 'Fitness trackers']

This simplified example mimics how an AI system might generate personalized recommendations based on user activity.

Challenges in Building AI Workflows

Building effective AI workflows isn't without challenges. Some common issues include:

1. Data Quality: Poor data can lead to unreliable outputs. Preprocessing is critical.
2. Integration Complexity: Connecting models, APIs, and databases can become complicated.
3. Real-Time Performance: Some workflows need to operate in real-time, requiring optimization.
4. Error Handling: The workflow must handle unexpected failures without breaking.
5. Scalability: A workflow that works for 10 users may not work for 10,000.

Addressing these challenges requires thoughtful design and the right tools, which is where frameworks like LangChain and LangGraph become essential.

Exercise: Design a Basic Workflow

Task:
Design a workflow for a virtual assistant that schedules meetings. It should:

1. Accept a meeting request.
2. Check the user's calendar (mock data).
3. Suggest an available time.

Hint:

- Define mock data for calendar availability.
- Write simple logic to suggest the next available time.

An AI workflow is more than just running a model—it's a coordinated process that takes input, processes it intelligently, and produces useful outputs. Whether you're building a chatbot, a recommendation system, or an automation tool, understanding how workflows are structured is the foundation for creating dynamic AI systems.

1.2 The Role of Autonomous Agents in AI

An autonomous agent is a system that can perceive its environment, make decisions, and take actions to achieve specific goals. What makes it autonomous is its ability to operate independently, without being told what to do at every step.

Key Characteristics of Autonomous Agents

1. Perception: The agent gathers data from its environment (user input, sensors, APIs).
2. Decision-Making: It processes information and decides what action to take.
3. Action: The agent performs tasks or communicates results.
4. Adaptation: It can learn and adjust its behavior based on past experiences.

Real-World Example: Smart Personal Assistants

Think about virtual assistants like Google Assistant or Amazon Alexa. These are autonomous agents because they:

- Listen to your voice commands (perception).

- Decide whether to search the web, control a smart device, or set a reminder (decision-making).
- Execute the task and provide feedback (action).
- Learn your preferences over time to offer more relevant suggestions (adaptation).

Types of Autonomous Agents

1. Reactive Agents: These agents respond directly to inputs without long-term memory or complex reasoning. Their behavior is predefined.

Example:
A thermostat that turns on heating when the temperature drops below a threshold.

2. Proactive Agents: These agents can anticipate future needs and take initiative. They analyze data to predict and act.

Example:
A calendar assistant that suggests leaving earlier for a meeting based on traffic predictions.

3. Hybrid Agents: These agents combine reactive and proactive behaviors. They can handle immediate inputs while also planning for future events.

Example:
An AI customer service agent that answers FAQs (reactive) but also follows up with personalized offers (proactive).

How Do Autonomous Agents Work?

An autonomous agent typically operates in a loop of sensing, thinking, and acting. Here's a simple cycle:

1. Sense (Perception): The agent receives input (text, voice, sensor data).

2. Think (Decision-Making): It processes the input and decides the next action.
3. Act (Execution): The agent performs the chosen action.
4. Learn (Optional): The agent updates its behavior based on outcomes.

Architecture of an Autonomous Agent

Let's break this down into components:

- Input Processor: Handles data from the environment.
- Reasoning Engine: Applies logic or models to make decisions.
- Action Executor: Executes the chosen action.
- Memory (Optional): Stores past interactions for learning and adaptation.

Building a Simple Autonomous Agent with LangChain

Let's build a basic autonomous agent that can answer questions and search for information when it doesn't know the answer.

Scenario:

The agent will first try to answer a question using its built-in knowledge. If it can't, it will search the web for an answer.

Code Example:

```
from langchain.agents import initialize_agent, Tool

from langchain.llms import OpenAI

from langchain.utilities import SerpAPIWrapper
```

```python
# Initialize the OpenAI language model
llm = OpenAI(temperature=0)


# Initialize a web search tool
search = SerpAPIWrapper()


# Define the tools the agent can use
tools = [
    Tool(
        name="Web Search",
        func=search.run,
        description="Use this tool to search the
web when you don't know the answer."
    )
]


# Initialize the autonomous agent with reasoning
ability
agent = initialize_agent(

                                tools,          llm,
agent_type="zero-shot-react-description",
verbose=True
```

```
)
```

```
# Test the agent with a question

question = "Who won the FIFA World Cup in 2022?"

response = agent.run(question)

print(response)
```

Explanation of the Workflow

1. Perception: The agent receives the question as input.
2. Decision-Making: It decides whether it knows the answer. If not, it uses the web search tool.
3. Action: The agent either answers the question directly or fetches the answer online.

This is a simple but effective example of an autonomous agent that can reason and select tools dynamically.

Expanding the Agent's Capabilities

To make agents more powerful, they need to handle more than just one tool. Let's add a calculator for math questions.

Updated Code with Multiple Tools:

```
from langchain.agents import Tool

from langchain.utilities import PythonREPL


# Add a Python REPL tool for calculations

calculator = PythonREPL()
```

```python
# Extend tools with a calculator

tools = [

    Tool(

        name="Web Search",

        func=search.run,

        description="Use this tool to search the
web."

    ),

    Tool(

        name="Calculator",

        func=calculator.run,

        description="Use this tool for math
calculations."

    )

]


# Re-initialize the agent with the new tool

agent = initialize_agent(

    tools, llm,
agent_type="zero-shot-react-description",
verbose=True
```

```
)


# Test the agent with a math question

math_question = "What is 1234 * 5678?"

response = agent.run(math_question)

print(response)
```

How This Agent Works:

- For factual questions, it uses web search.
- For math problems, it automatically switches to the calculator.

This is autonomy in action. The agent decides how to solve a problem and selects the best tool for the job.

Real-World Application: Autonomous AI in Business

Let's apply this concept to a practical scenario.

Scenario: Customer Support Automation

Problem: A business receives hundreds of customer inquiries daily. Simple questions should be answered automatically, but complex issues need to be escalated.

Solution: Deploy an autonomous agent with three abilities:

1. Answer FAQs using an internal knowledge base.
2. Process Refunds by integrating with a payment system.
3. Escalate Complaints to human agents when necessary.

Workflow:

1. Input: A customer sends a message.
2. Decision: The agent classifies the request as a FAQ, refund, or complaint.
3. Action:
    - o   For FAQs: Respond automatically.
    - o   For refunds: Trigger a refund process.
    - o   For complaints: Forward to human support.

High-Level Pseudocode:

```
def handle_customer_request(request):

    if is_faq(request):

        return answer_faq(request)

    elif is_refund_request(request):

        return process_refund(request)

    else:

        return escalate_to_human(request)



# Simulate a request

customer_request = "I need a refund for my last
order."

response =
handle_customer_request(customer_request)

print(response)
```

Challenges in Building Autonomous Agents

1. Decision Accuracy: The agent must correctly interpret inputs and choose the right action.
2. Error Handling: It must handle failures gracefully (e.g., failed API calls).
3. Security and Privacy: Agents interacting with sensitive data need strict security measures.
4. Adaptability: Agents must adapt to new tasks without requiring complete rewrites.

These challenges highlight why designing autonomous agents requires thoughtful planning and robust tools like LangChain.

Exercise: Build a Task Management Agent

Objective:
Create an autonomous agent that:

1. Accepts a task (e.g., "Schedule a meeting at 3 PM").
2. Checks for time conflicts.
3. Confirms or rescheduled the meeting.

Hints:

- Define a mock calendar.
- Use decision logic to check availability.

Autonomous agents are the backbone of intelligent AI systems. They can perceive their environment, make decisions, and act independently to solve problems. Whether it's a chatbot answering questions, a recommendation engine suggesting products, or a business automation tool handling tasks, autonomous agents make AI systems more flexible and powerful.

1.3 Challenges in Building Dynamic AI Systems

Building dynamic AI systems is an exciting yet complex task. Unlike traditional software systems that follow static, predefined workflows, dynamic AI systems must adapt to changing conditions, handle diverse inputs, make decisions in real-time, and interact with multiple tools and data sources. This adaptability introduces significant challenges that must be carefully managed.

In this section, we'll discuss these challenges in detail and discuss practical solutions. You'll also find real-world examples and complete working code to help you understand how to address these challenges effectively.

1. Complexity in Integration of Multiple Components

One of the most significant challenges in building dynamic AI systems is integrating various components—machine learning models, APIs, databases, and external tools—into a single, cohesive system. Each component might have its own interface, data format, and operational constraints.

Real-World Example:

Consider building a virtual assistant that can:

- Answer general knowledge questions.
- Schedule meetings by checking a calendar.
- Send notifications via email.

Each task requires integrating different services: a language model, a calendar API, and an email server. Ensuring these systems work together smoothly is a non-trivial task.

Common Issues:

- Incompatible Data Formats: Data flowing between components may require complex transformations.
- Error Propagation: A failure in one service can cascade and break the entire system.
- Latency: Delays in one service can slow down the whole workflow.

Solution:

Use a workflow orchestration tool like LangChain to handle the communication between components. Let's create a small example that integrates a language model with a scheduling function.

Code Example: Integrating a Chatbot with a Scheduler

```
from langchain import OpenAI, LLMChain

from datetime import datetime


# Initialize the language model

llm = OpenAI(temperature=0)


# Simple scheduler function

def check_calendar():

    busy_hours = [10, 14, 16]   # Mocked busy
hours

    available_hours = [hour for hour in range(9,
18) if hour not in busy_hours]

    return available_hours
```

```python
# Workflow to schedule a meeting

def schedule_meeting(request):

    available_hours = check_calendar()

    if available_hours:

        return f"Available slots are:
{available_hours}"

    else:

        return "No available slots today."



# Test the system

user_request = "Can you schedule a meeting for
me?"

response = schedule_meeting(user_request)

print(response)
```

Output:

Available slots are: [9, 11, 12, 13, 15, 17]

Explanation:
  Here, the system checks the calendar and suggests available time slots. This is a simple example, but it demonstrates how components can work together.

2. Real-Time Decision-Making

Dynamic AI systems often need to make decisions on the fly. Real-time decision-making requires processing incoming data, evaluating options, and selecting the best course of action without significant delays.

Real-World Example:

A self-driving car must process sensor data, detect objects, predict their movement, and make navigation decisions—all in milliseconds.

Challenges:

- Data Volume: Processing large amounts of data quickly.
- Latency Sensitivity: Even slight delays can cause failures.
- Uncertainty Handling: Decisions must be made with incomplete information.

Solution:

Implement lightweight decision-making models or rule-based logic for critical tasks, while delegating complex reasoning to larger models when time allows.

3. Context and Memory Management

For AI systems to feel intelligent, they must maintain context throughout interactions. Without memory, an AI system can't understand the flow of conversation or past actions.

Real-World Example:

A customer service chatbot should remember that a user previously asked about shipping delays when responding to follow-up questions.

Challenges:

- Memory Overload: Too much information can slow down processing.
- Context Switching: Handling multiple users or tasks simultaneously.
- State Persistence: Keeping memory consistent across sessions.

Solution:

Use LangChain's Memory modules to store and manage state across interactions.

Code Example: Contextual Memory in a Chatbot

```
from langchain.chains import ConversationChain

from langchain.memory import
ConversationBufferMemory



# Initialize conversation memory

memory = ConversationBufferMemory()



# Create a conversational AI with memory

conversation = ConversationChain(

    llm=OpenAI(temperature=0),

    memory=memory

)
```

```
# Simulate conversation

print(conversation.run("Hi, I need help with my
order."))

print(conversation.run("When will it arrive?"))
```

Expected Output:

AI: Sure! Can you provide your order number?

AI: Based on your order, it should arrive in 3-5 business days.

Explanation:
 The agent remembers the previous context, so it understands that the user is asking about the order in the second question.

4. Error Handling and System Robustness

No system is perfect. APIs fail, network issues occur, and models sometimes produce errors. Without proper error handling, these failures can cripple the entire system.

Real-World Example:

If an AI customer support agent fails to process a refund due to a payment API error, it should notify the user and attempt a retry.

Challenges:

- Service Downtime: External APIs might become unavailable.
- Invalid Inputs: Unexpected inputs can break workflows.
- Error Propagation: Failures in one part can affect others.

Solution:

Implement retry mechanisms and graceful fallbacks.

Code Example: Adding Error Handling

```python
import requests


def get_weather(city):
    try:
        response = requests.get(f"https://api.weatherapi.com/{city}")

        response.raise_for_status()

        return response.json()
    except requests.RequestException as e:
        return f"Error fetching weather data: {e}"


# Test with a faulty API call
print(get_weather("New York"))
```

Explanation:
If the API fails, the system gracefully handles the error instead of crashing.

5. Scalability and Performance Optimization

As the user base grows, AI systems must scale without degrading performance. Systems that work with ten users may struggle with ten thousand.

Real-World Example:

An AI-powered e-commerce recommendation system must handle millions of users during holiday sales.

Challenges:

- Resource Constraints: Limited memory and CPU/GPU power.
- Concurrency: Handling multiple requests simultaneously.
- Model Serving: Scaling model inference under heavy load.

Solution:

- Asynchronous processing to handle multiple tasks.
- Caching for frequently requested data.
- Load balancing across servers.

Exercise: Error Handling in a Workflow

Task:
Expand the meeting scheduler example to handle errors when the calendar service is down. If the service fails, it should notify the user gracefully.

Building dynamic AI systems involves navigating several challenges, including complex integrations, real-time decision-making, memory management, error handling, and scalability. Each of these challenges requires thoughtful solutions and robust engineering practices.

The good news is that with tools like **LangChain** and **LangGraph**, many of these issues can be handled more effectively. As we move forward, we'll explore how these frameworks help simplify and streamline the process of building dynamic, intelligent systems.

1.4 Introduction to LangChain and LangGraph

Dynamic AI systems demand more than just a powerful model—they require structured workflows that can reason, interact with tools, access external data, and adapt to new information in real-time. This is where LangChain and LangGraph come into play. These two frameworks provide the foundation for building intelligent, scalable, and adaptable AI systems.

What Is LangChain?

LangChain is a powerful Python framework designed to simplify the development of applications powered by large language models (LLMs). It allows developers to build complex AI workflows by connecting LLMs with external tools, data sources, and APIs.

Large language models like GPT-4 are impressive but limited when used alone. They can generate text, answer questions, and summarize content, but they cannot:

- Retrieve real-time data.
- Perform calculations.
- Access databases or APIs.

LangChain solves this by bridging the gap between language models and external resources. It allows LLMs to interact with external tools and make intelligent decisions in dynamic workflows.

Key Features of LangChain

1. Chains: Define sequences of tasks that the model can execute.
2. Agents: Enable dynamic decision-making by choosing the right tool for the job.

3. Tools Integration: Seamlessly connect the model to APIs, databases, search engines, and more.
4. Memory: Allow the model to retain context across multiple interactions.
5. Prompt Management: Simplify the design and handling of prompts.

What Is LangGraph?

While LangChain structures workflows linearly (step-by-step), LangGraph introduces graph-based workflows. In LangGraph, tasks are structured as interconnected nodes and edges, allowing for non-linear, dynamic, and adaptive task execution.

Some AI workflows can't be built as simple sequences—they need to handle decision branches, loops, and parallel processes. LangGraph allows developers to:

- Create complex workflows with conditional logic.
- Manage branching and looping processes.
- Handle failure points with fallback paths.

Key Features of LangGraph

1. Graph-Based Execution: Define workflows as graphs with nodes (tasks) and edges (transitions).
2. Dynamic Logic: Easily handle conditional flows and branching logic.
3. Error Handling: Create fallback paths for handling errors or unexpected inputs.
4. Parallel Processing: Run multiple tasks simultaneously when needed.

LangChain in Action: A Simple Use Case

Let's start with a basic example. We'll build a LangChain-based AI that can generate answers to user queries.

Problem:

You want to create a system that can generate articles on any topic.

Solution:

Use LangChain to connect a language model to a prompt that asks the model to generate content.

Code Example: Simple LangChain Workflow

```python
from langchain import OpenAI, LLMChain

from langchain.prompts import PromptTemplate


# Step 1: Define a prompt template
prompt = PromptTemplate(

    input_variables=["topic"],

    template="Write a 200-word article about {topic}."

)


# Step 2: Initialize the language model
llm_chain = LLMChain(llm=OpenAI(temperature=0.7),
prompt=prompt)


# Step 3: Generate content
topic = "Artificial Intelligence in Healthcare"
```

```
response = llm_chain.run(topic)

print(response)
```

Explanation:

- **PromptTemplate:** We define how to interact with the model using a structured prompt.
- **LLMChain:** The model uses this prompt to generate content.
- **Result:** The model generates an article on the requested topic.

This is a basic example of a **chain**—a linear sequence of steps. But what if the workflow needs to adapt based on the user's input? That's where agents come in.

LangChain Agents: Adding Intelligence to Workflows

Agents in LangChain allow AI systems to make decisions dynamically. Instead of following a fixed sequence, agents choose the right tools to solve a problem based on the context.

Real-World Example:

Let's build a smart assistant that:

- Answers general questions.
- Uses a calculator for math problems.
- Searches the web for unknown answers.

Code Example: LangChain Agent with Multiple Tools

```
from langchain.agents import initialize_agent, Tool

from langchain.llms import OpenAI

from langchain.utilities import SerpAPIWrapper
```

```python
from langchain.utilities import PythonREPL


# Initialize the LLM

llm = OpenAI(temperature=0)


# Define tools

search_tool = SerpAPIWrapper()

calculator_tool = PythonREPL()


tools = [

    Tool(name="Web Search", func=search_tool.run,
description="Use for general search queries."),

    Tool(name="Calculator", func=calculator_tool.run,
description="Use for math problems.")

]


# Initialize the agent

agent = initialize_agent(tools, llm,
agent_type="zero-shot-react-description", verbose=True)


# Test the agent

response = agent.run("What is 45 * 67?")

print(response)
```

Explanation:

- **Tools:** We defined a web search and calculator tool.
- **Agent:** The agent decides which tool to use based on the input.
- **Result:** For a math problem, it uses the calculator. For general queries, it searches the web.

This is a flexible system that can dynamically decide how to handle different tasks.

LangGraph in Action: Complex Decision-Making

For workflows that involve branching logic and error handling, LangGraph is more suitable. Let's create a workflow that:

- Starts with a user query.
- Checks if the query can be answered by the model.
- If not, searches the web for an answer.
- If both fail, respond with an error message.

Conceptual Graph Workflow:

1. Start Node: Receive user input.
2. Decision Node: Can the model answer the question?
3. Action Node: If yes, generate the answer. If not, use web search.
4. Error Node: If both fail, send an apology message.

Pseudocode Example:

```
# Pseudocode for a graph-based workflow


def answer_query(query):

    if model_can_answer(query):
```

```
    return model_answer(query)

  elif web_search_can_answer(query):

    return web_search_answer(query)

  else:

    return "Sorry, I couldn't find an answer."



# Example usage

response = answer_query("What is the capital of France?")

print(response)
```

This flow is much easier to design and manage using LangGraph because it naturally supports branching logic.

When to Use LangChain vs. LangGraph

Feature	LangChain	LangGraph
Workflow Type	Linear and sequential tasks	Complex, branching, and adaptive tasks
Best for	Simple chains and agents	Dynamic decision-making and error handling

Error Handling	Requires manual handling	Built-in through fallback paths
Parallel Processing	Limited	Natively supported

Exercise: Build a Smart Assistant

Objective:
Create an AI assistant that:

1. Answers factual questions.
2. Performs math calculations.
3. Apologies if it cannot handle the request.

Hint:

- Use LangChain for tool integration.
- Add error handling for unknown inputs.

LangChain simplifies the process of building intelligent, tool-augmented AI applications. It allows language models to interact with APIs, databases, and even execute code. LangGraph extends this capability by enabling complex, graph-based workflows with dynamic decision-making, branching, and error handling.

1.5 Key Concepts and Terminology

Before we go into building dynamic AI systems using LangChain and LangGraph, it's critical to understand the foundational concepts and terminology that will guide the entire development process. This section will give you a clear and thorough understanding of these core ideas, with practical examples and real-world relevance.

Let's break down these concepts one by one, ensuring you have the tools and knowledge to build powerful and intelligent AI workflows.

1. Chain

A Chain in LangChain is a sequence of actions where the output of one step becomes the input for the next. It's similar to a pipeline where data flows through a series of transformations or tasks to achieve a goal.

Real-World Example:

Think about a customer support chatbot. The workflow might be:

1. Input: Receive a customer query.
2. Processing: Analyze the intent of the message.
3. Action: Provide a relevant response or escalate to a human.

Code Example: Simple Chain

```python
from langchain import OpenAI, LLMChain

from langchain.prompts import PromptTemplate


# Step 1. Define a prompt template

prompt = PromptTemplate(

    input_variables=["product"],

    template="Write a product description for {product}."
```

```
)
```

```
# Step 2: Initialize the language model chain

llm_chain = LLMChain(llm=OpenAI(temperature=0.7),
prompt=prompt)
```

```
# Step 3: Run the chain

response = llm_chain.run("wireless headphones")

print(response)
```

Explanation:

- PromptTemplate: Defines the task (writing a product description).
- LLMChain: Connects the task to the language model.
- Result: The model generates a product description for "wireless headphones."

2. Agent

An Agent is a more advanced concept than a chain. While a chain follows a fixed path, an agent makes decisions dynamically. It can choose which tools or actions to use depending on the input.

Real-World Example:

A virtual assistant that can:

- Answer FAQs from a knowledge base.
- Perform calculations.
- Search the web when it doesn't know the answer.

Code Example: Agent with Multiple Tools

```python
from langchain.agents import initialize_agent, Tool

from langchain.llms import OpenAI

from langchain.utilities import SerpAPIWrapper

from langchain.utilities import PythonREPL


# Initialize the language model

llm = OpenAI(temperature=0)


# Define tools for the agent

search_tool = SerpAPIWrapper()

calculator_tool = PythonREPL()


tools = [

    Tool(name="Web Search", func=search_tool.run,
description="Search the web."),

    Tool(name="Calculator", func=calculator_tool.run,
description="Perform math operations.")

]


# Initialize the agent with decision-making abilities

agent = initialize_agent(tools, llm,
agent_type="zero-shot-react-description", verbose=True)


# Run the agent
```

```
response = agent.run("What is 42 * 13?")

print(response)
```

Explanation:

- Tools: The agent has access to both a web search tool and a calculator.
- Agent: Decides which tool to use. For a math question, it chooses the calculator

3. Tool

A Tool is an external function or service that the agent can use to accomplish a task. Tools can be APIs, databases, search engines, or even custom Python functions.

Real-World Example:

- Calculator: Performs arithmetic operations.
- Database Query: Fetches data from a database.
- Web Scraper: Extracts real-time data from websites.

Code Example: Custom Tool

```
def custom_greeting(name):

    return f"Hello, {name}! How can I help you
today?"



# Define the tool

greeting_tool = Tool(name="Greeting",
func=custom_greeting, description="Greets the user.")



# Use the tool
```

```
print(greeting_tool.run("Alex"))
```

Output:

Hello, Alex! How can I help you today?

Explanation:
This custom tool greets users by name, showing how flexible tools can be in LangChain.

4. Memory

Memory allows an agent to remember previous interactions, making conversations more natural and context-aware. Without memory, every input is treated in isolation.

Real-World Example:

In a customer support chatbot, if a user says, "I want to track my order," and later asks, "When will it arrive?" the bot should remember the initial request.

Code Example: Conversation Memory

```
from langchain.chains import ConversationChain

from langchain.memory import ConversationBufferMemory


# Initialize memory

memory = ConversationBufferMemory()


# Create a conversation chain with memory

conversation = ConversationChain(llm=OpenAI(temperature=0),
memory=memory)
```

```
# Simulate conversation

print(conversation.run("Hi, I need help with my order."))

print(conversation.run("When will it arrive?"))
```

Output:

AI: Sure! Can you provide your order number?

AI: Based on your order, it should arrive in 3-5 business days.

Explanation:
The AI remembers that the user is asking about an order, enabling it to respond appropriately.

5. Node (LangGraph)

In LangGraph, a Node represents a task or decision point in a workflow. Nodes are the building blocks of graph-based workflows.

Real-World Example:

In a fraud detection system:

- Node 1: Analyze transaction data.
- Node 2: Check user behavior.
- Node 3: Flag as fraud or approve.

6. Edge (LangGraph)

An Edge is a connection between nodes in a LangGraph workflow. It defines how the system moves from one task to another based on certain conditions.

Real-World Example:

If a transaction is flagged as suspicious (Node 2), the workflow transitions to manual review (Node 3).

7. Prompt Template

A Prompt Template is a reusable structure for generating model inputs. It ensures consistent, well-structured prompts.

Code Example: Prompt Template

```
from langchain.prompts import PromptTemplate



# Define a template

template = PromptTemplate(

    input_variables=["topic"],

    template="Explain the concept of {topic} in simple
terms."

)



# Use the template

prompt = template.format(topic="machine learning")

print(prompt)
```

Output:

Explain the concept of machine learning in simple terms.

Chain vs. Agent

Feature	Chain	Agent
Workflow Type	Fixed and linear	Dynamic and adaptable
Decision-Making	No (predefined steps)	Yes (chooses tools dynamically)
Complexity	Simple to moderate	Moderate to complex
Use Case	Predictable tasks (content generation)	Variable tasks (chatbots, automation)

Exercise: Build a Simple Workflow

Task:
Create a LangChain workflow that:

1. Greetings to the user.
2. Calculates the square of a number.
3. Apologizes if the input isn't a number.

Hint:

- Use a Tool for the calculator.

- Add error handling for invalid inputs.

Understanding these key concepts—Chains, Agents, Tools, Memory, Nodes, and Edges—is crucial for building effective AI systems. LangChain simplifies the creation of structured workflows, while LangGraph allows for dynamic, complex, and adaptive processes.

Chapter 2: Getting Started with LangChain

In this chapter, we will walk through everything you need to get started with LangChain. You'll gain a deep understanding of its architecture, learn how to set up your development environment, explore its core components, and build your very first LangChain workflow. By the end of this chapter, you'll have a solid foundation to start creating powerful and dynamic AI workflows.

2.1 Setting Up the Development Environment

In this section, I'll guide you step-by-step through installing the necessary tools, configuring API keys, and verifying that everything works correctly. By the end, you'll be ready to start building LangChain applications confidently.

Step 1: Install Python

LangChain is a Python-based framework. To get started, you need Python 3.8 or later.

Check if Python is Installed

Open your terminal (Command Prompt on Windows or Terminal on macOS/Linux) and run:

```
python --version
```

If Python is installed, you'll see something like:

Python 3.10.6

If Python isn't installed, download it from the official website:
https://www.python.org/downloads/

Install Python (if needed)

Follow the installation steps for your operating system. On Windows, make sure to check "Add Python to PATH" during installation.

To verify that Python and pip (Python's package installer) are working:

```
pip --version
```

If this shows a version number, you're good to go.

Step 2: Set Up a Virtual Environment

Using a virtual environment keeps your project's dependencies isolated and avoids version conflicts between packages.

Create a Virtual Environment

In your project folder, run:

```
python -m venv langchain_env
```

This creates a new folder named langchain_env that contains an isolated Python environment.

Activate the Virtual Environment

- Windows:

```
langchain_env\Scripts\activate
```

- macOS/Linux:

```
source langchain_env/bin/activate
```

Once activated, your terminal will show (langchain_env) at the start of the command line.

Step 3: Install LangChain and Dependencies

Now, let's install LangChain and its required packages.

Install LangChain

```
pip install langchain
```

Install Common Dependencies

LangChain works best with certain libraries for connecting to models and tools. Install these as well:

```
pip install openai python-dotenv serpapi
```

Explanation:

- openai: Connects to OpenAI models like GPT-3.
- python-dotenv: Safely loads API keys from environment files.
- serpapi: Enables web search capability.

Verify Installation

Run Python and import LangChain to ensure it's installed:

```
python
```

```
from langchain import OpenAI
```

If no errors appear, the installation was successful. Type exit() to close Python.

Step 4: Configure API Keys

LangChain interacts with external services like OpenAI and SerpAPI. For security, we store these keys in a .env file.

```
Create a .env File

In your project folder, create a file named .env:

touch .env


Add the following to the .env file:

OPENAI_API_KEY=your_openai_api_key

SERPAPI_API_KEY=your_serpapi_api_key


Load API Keys in Python

Install and use python-dotenv to load these keys:

from dotenv import load_dotenv

import os


# Load the .env file

load_dotenv()


# Access API keys

openai_api_key = os.getenv("OPENAI_API_KEY")

serpapi_api_key = os.getenv("SERPAPI_API_KEY")


print(f"OpenAI Key: {openai_api_key}")
```

```
print(f"SerpAPI Key: {serpapi_api_key}")
```

Explanation:
 This script safely loads your API keys so they aren't hard coded into your programs.

Step 5: Test Your Setup

Let's run a basic LangChain workflow to confirm that everything is working.

Code Example: Generate Text with OpenAI

```
from langchain import OpenAI

# Initialize the OpenAI model

llm = OpenAI(temperature=0.7)



# Generate text

response = llm("Explain the benefits of using AI in education.")

print(response)
```

Expected Output:
 A few sentences explaining how AI can enhance educational systems.

Explanation:
 If this script runs without error and produces a meaningful output, LangChain and OpenAI are correctly set up.

Step 6: Install Optional Development Tools

To improve your coding experience, install some additional tools.

Jupyter Notebook (Optional)

For interactive development, Jupyter Notebook is a great tool:

```
pip install notebook
```

Run Jupyter Notebook:

```
jupyter notebook
```

VS Code (Recommended)

If you're using Visual Studio Code, install the Python extension for code linting, auto-completion, and debugging.

Step 7: Troubleshooting Common Issues

1. OpenAI API Error

If you see:

InvalidRequestError: No API key provided.

Fix:

- Double-check that your .env file has the correct API key.
- Ensure you loaded the environment variables with load_dotenv().

2. Module Not Found Error

If Python can't find a module like LangChain:

ModuleNotFoundError: No module named 'langchain'

Fix:

- Ensure your virtual environment is activated.
- Reinstall the package: pip install langchain

3. Network Errors

If external APIs aren't working:

Fix:

- Check your internet connection.
- Ensure your API keys are correct and active.

Exercise: Build a Quick Tool

Objective:
Test your setup by building a simple LangChain tool that generates a fun fact about any topic.

Code Example: Fun Fact Generator

```
from langchain import OpenAI

from langchain.prompts import PromptTemplate



# Initialize the model

llm = OpenAI(temperature=0.7)



# Create a prompt

prompt = PromptTemplate(

    input_variables=["topic"],

    template="Tell me an interesting fact about {topic}."
```

```
)

# Generate a fun fact

topic = "space exploration"

response = llm(prompt.format(topic=topic))

print(response)
```

Expected Output:
An interesting fact about space exploration!

By completing this setup, you've laid a strong foundation for building intelligent applications with LangChain. You've:

- Installed Python and dependencies.
- Configured API keys securely.
- Tested LangChain with a working example.

This environment is now ready to support more advanced workflows and tools. In the next section, we'll explore LangChain's core components—**Chains**, **Tools**, and **Prompts**—and how they work together to build powerful AI systems.

2.2 Core Components

To build dynamic and intelligent AI systems with LangChain, you need to master its core components: **Chains, Tools**, and **Prompts**. These are the foundational building blocks that allow you to design flexible, multi-step workflows capable of handling complex tasks. In this section, I will explain each of these components in detail, show you how they work together, and provide real-world examples along with complete, working code. This will ensure you gain both theoretical understanding and practical experience.

1. Chains

A Chain in LangChain is a sequence of connected steps that process input and produce output. Each step can involve models, tools, or data processing functions. Think of it as a pipeline where data flows from one step to the next.

Chains allow you to structure workflows in a clean, modular way, making it easier to manage complex tasks.

Why Are Chains Important?

- Reusability: Chains can be broken into reusable steps.
- Flexibility: They can be as simple or complex as needed.
- Scalability: You can easily add more steps as requirements grow.

Basic Chain Example: Generating a Blog Post Title

Let's start with a simple example. We'll create a chain that generates a blog post title for a given topic.

```
from langchain import OpenAI, LLMChain

from langchain.prompts import PromptTemplate


# Initialize the language model

llm = OpenAI(temperature=0.7)


# Define a prompt template

prompt = PromptTemplate(

    input_variables=["topic"],
```

```python
    template="Suggest a creative blog post title about {topic}."

)
```

```python
# Create a chain that combines the model and the prompt

chain = LLMChain(llm=llm, prompt=prompt)
```

```python
# Run the chain

response = chain.run("Artificial Intelligence in Healthcare")

print(response)
```

Expected Output:

"Revolutionizing Healthcare: How AI is Shaping the Future of Medicine"

Explanation:

- The prompt provides structured input.
- The model generates text based on the prompt.
- The chain connects these steps into a workflow.

2. Tools

Tools are external functions or APIs that the AI can use to perform specialized tasks. They extend the model's capabilities beyond text generation.

Why Are Tools Important?

- **Extend Functionality: Perform tasks models alone can't handle.**
- **Access Real-Time Data: Retrieve live information (e.g., web search).**
- **Integrate Systems:** Connect to APIs, databases, or custom functions.

Tool Example: Using a Calculator

Let's integrate a simple calculator as a tool. The model will use this tool to solve math problems.

```
from langchain.utilities import PythonREPL
```

```
# Initialize a Python REPL tool (acts as a calculator)

calculator = PythonREPL()
```

```
# Run a calculation

result = calculator.run("45 * 3 + 12")

print(result)
```

Expected Output:

147

Explanation:

- The PythonREPL tool evaluates the expression.
- Tools like this offload specialized tasks from the model.

Combining Tools with Agents

Tools become even more powerful when combined with agents, which can decide which tool to use based on the input.

Example: If a user asks for a calculation, the agent should use the calculator. If the user asks a general question, the agent should use the language model.

```
from langchain.agents import initialize_agent,
Tool


# Define the calculator tool

tools = [

    Tool(name="Calculator", func=calculator.run,
description="Performs math operations.")

]


# Initialize the agent with the tool

agent = initialize_agent(tools, llm,
agent_type="zero-shot-react-description")


# Run the agent

response = agent.run("What is 15 * 7?")

print(response)
```

Expected Output:

105

Explanation:
The agent intelligently decides to use the calculator tool to solve the math problem.

3. Prompts

Prompts are the instructions you give to a language model. Well-crafted prompts guide the model to generate the desired output.

Why Are Prompts Important?

- **Control the Output:** Models only generate as good as the prompts they receive.
- **Consistency:** Structured prompts lead to more reliable results.
- **Customization:** Tailor responses for specific tasks.

Prompt Template Example: Writing Product Descriptions

Let's create a prompt that generates product descriptions for an e-commerce website.

```
from langchain.prompts import PromptTemplate
```

```
# Define a prompt template for product
descriptions

prompt = PromptTemplate(

    input_variables=["product"],

    template="Write a compelling product
description for {product}."
```

```
)
```

```
# Format the prompt

formatted_prompt =
prompt.format(product="Wireless Noise-Canceling
Headphones")

print(formatted_prompt)
```

Expected Output:

Write a compelling product description for Wireless Noise-Canceling Headphones.

Explanation:

- PromptTemplate allows for dynamic input.
- You can easily change the product to generate different descriptions.

Combining Prompts with Models

Now, let's use this prompt with a model to generate the product description.

```
# Create a chain using the prompt and model

description_chain = LLMChain(llm=llm,
prompt=prompt)
```

```
# Generate a product description

response = description_chain.run("Wireless
Noise-Canceling Headphones")
```

```
print(response)
```

Expected Output:

Experience pure, uninterrupted sound with our Wireless Noise-Canceling Headphones. Designed for comfort and clarity, these headphones deliver crystal-clear audio and block out background noise, making them perfect for work, travel, and relaxation.

Explanation:

- The prompt gives structure to the model's input.
- The chain connects the prompt and model to produce the final output.

Putting It All Together

Let's create a more complex workflow that combines Chains, Tools, and Prompts.

Problem:

Design an AI assistant that:

1. Answers general questions.
2. Calculates math problems.
3. Writes product descriptions.

Complete Code Example: Multi-Function AI Assistant

```
from langchain.agents import initialize_agent,
Tool

from langchain.prompts import PromptTemplate


# Define a prompt for product descriptions
```

```python
product_prompt = PromptTemplate(

    input_variables=["product"],

    template="Write an engaging product
description for {product}."

)


# Create a product description chain

product_chain = LLMChain(llm=llm,
prompt=product_prompt)


# Define the tools

tools = [

    Tool(name="Calculator", func=calculator.run,
description="Handles math problems."),

    Tool(name="Product Description",
func=product_chain.run, description="Writes
product descriptions.")

]


# Initialize the agent

assistant_agent = initialize_agent(tools, llm,
agent_type="zero-shot-react-description")
```

```
# Test the assistant with different tasks

print(assistant_agent.run("What is 24 * 5?"))

print(assistant_agent.run("Describe a new
smartwatch."))
```

Expected Output:

120

Introducing our latest smartwatch: a sleek, modern design packed with health tracking features, real-time notifications, and long battery life. Stay connected and active with cutting-edge technology on your wrist.

Explanation:

- Agent: Decides which tool to use based on the query.
- Calculator Tool: Solves the math problem.
- Product Chain: Generates the product description.

Exercise: Create Your Own Workflow

Task:
Build a LangChain workflow that:

1. Provides fun facts about any topic.
2. Calculates square roots.
3. Writes short poems on request.

Hint:

- Use Prompts for the fun fact and poem generator.
- Use the PythonREPL tool for calculations.

By mastering Chains, Tools, and Prompts, you can create powerful and flexible AI systems. These components allow you to:

- Structure workflows with Chains.
- Extend functionality with Tools.
- Guide the model's behavior with well-designed Prompts.

These are the foundational skills you need to build more complex, dynamic workflows. In the next section, we will explore how to connect your AI systems to external APIs and data sources for real-time, data-driven intelligence.

2.3 Connecting to External APIs and Data Sources

Dynamic AI systems need to do more than just generate text. They must interact with external data sources and APIs to fetch real-time information, perform complex calculations, or access proprietary data. This ability makes AI systems more useful, adaptable, and relevant to real-world applications. In this section, we will explore how to connect LangChain applications to external APIs and data sources. I'll walk you through the process step-by-step, explain why each step matters, and provide complete working code examples to solidify your understanding.

Why Connect to External APIs and Data Sources?

Large Language Models (LLMs) are powerful, but they have limitations:

1. Static Knowledge – They can't access real-time information.
2. Limited Capabilities – They can't perform specialized tasks like currency conversion or weather updates.
3. No Direct Data Access – They can't connect to databases or proprietary systems on their own.

By connecting to external APIs and data sources, we can:

- Provide Real-Time Information: Get live weather data, stock prices, or news.
- Access Specialized Tools: Perform calculations, analyze images, or retrieve data.
- Enhance Decision-Making: Pull in contextual data to improve AI responses.

Step 1: Choosing the Right API

Before connecting to an API, it's important to choose one that meets your application's needs. APIs come in many forms:

- Public APIs: OpenWeather, NewsAPI, or currency exchange APIs.
- Private APIs: Internal company APIs or proprietary services.
- Third-Party Tools: Specialized services like SerpAPI for search or Twilio for messaging.

For this section, I'll demonstrate how to connect to two popular APIs:

1. OpenWeather API – For fetching weather data.
2. SerpAPI – For performing web searches.

Step 2: Setting Up API Access

Most APIs require authentication through API keys. Storing these securely is critical for protecting sensitive information.

Installing Required Libraries

Let's start by installing the necessary Python packages:

```
pip install langchain python-dotenv requests
serpapi
```

- langchain: Core framework.
- python-dotenv: For managing environment variables.
- requests: For making HTTP requests.
- serpapi: For web search functionality.

Storing API Keys Securely

Create a .env file in your project directory:

```
touch .env
```

Add your API keys:

```
OPENWEATHER_API_KEY=your_openweather_api_key

SERPAPI_API_KEY=your_serpapi_api_key
```

Loading API Keys in Python

```
from dotenv import load_dotenv

import os


# Load environment variables from .env file

load_dotenv()


# Access the keys

openweather_api_key =
os.getenv("OPENWEATHER_API_KEY")
```

```
serpapi_api_key = os.getenv("SERPAPI_API_KEY")
```

```
print(f"OpenWeather API Key:
{openweather_api_key}")
```

```
print(f"SerpAPI API Key: {serpapi_api_key}")
```

Explanation:
This ensures your sensitive keys are not hardcoded and can be managed securely.

Step 3: Connecting to External APIs

Example 1: Fetching Real-Time Weather Data with OpenWeather API

Let's create a LangChain tool that retrieves live weather data.

```
import requests
```

```python
def get_weather(city):

    base_url =
"http://api.openweathermap.org/data/2.5/weather"

    params = {

        'q': city,

        'appid': openweather_api_key,

        'units': 'metric'

    }
```

```python
    response = requests.get(base_url,
params=params)

    if response.status_code == 200:

        data = response.json()

        weather =
data['weather'][0]['description']

        temp = data['main']['temp']

        return f"The weather in {city} is
{weather} with a temperature of {temp}°C."

    else:

        return "Sorry, I couldn't retrieve the
weather data."



# Test the function

print(get_weather("New York"))
```

Expected Output:

The weather in New York has a clear sky with a temperature of 22°C.

Explanation:

- We make a GET request to the OpenWeather API.
- The function extracts weather conditions and temperature.
- This data can now be used in any AI workflow.

Example 2: Web Search Integration with SerpAPI

Now, let's integrate SerpAPI to perform web searches.

```
from langchain.utilities import SerpAPIWrapper


# Initialize SerpAPI

search = SerpAPIWrapper()


# Perform a search

query = "Latest news on artificial intelligence"

result = search.run(query)

print(result)
```

Expected Output:
A summary or snippet of the latest news articles on artificial intelligence.

Explanation:

- SerpAPI fetches real-time search results.
- This allows AI systems to access current events and trends.

Step 4: Combining APIs with LangChain Agents

Now, let's combine these APIs into a dynamic LangChain agent that can answer questions and provide weather updates.

Complete Code Example: Multi-Function AI Assistant

```
from langchain import OpenAI

from langchain.agents import initialize_agent,
Tool
```

```python
# Initialize the language model

llm = OpenAI(temperature=0.7)


# Define a weather tool

weather_tool = Tool(

    name="Weather",

    func=get_weather,

    description="Provides the current weather for
a given city."

)


# Define a search tool

search_tool = Tool(

    name="Web Search",

    func=search.run,

    description="Searches the web for up-to-date
information."

)


# Combine tools
```

```
tools = [weather_tool, search_tool]
```

```
# Initialize the agent
```

```
assistant = initialize_agent(tools, llm,
agent_type="zero-shot-react-description")
```

```
# Test the agent
```

```
print(assistant.run("What's the weather like in
London?"))
```

```
print(assistant.run("Tell me the latest updates
on electric vehicles."))
```

Expected Output:

The weather in London is cloudy with a temperature of 15°C.

Here are the latest updates on electric vehicles: [News snippet from the web]

Explanation:

- The agent decides which tool to use.
- For weather questions, it calls the OpenWeather API.
- For general queries, it performs a web search.

Step 5: Error Handling

APIs can fail due to network issues, invalid inputs, or server errors. Let's add basic error handling.

```
def get_weather(city):
```

```
try:

        response =
requests.get(f"http://api.openweathermap.org/data
/2.5/weather?q={city}&appid={openweather_api_key}
&units=metric")

        response.raise_for_status()

        data = response.json()

        weather =
data['weather'][0]['description']

        temp = data['main']['temp']

        return f"The weather in {city} is
{weather} with a temperature of {temp}°C."

    except requests.exceptions.HTTPError as
http_err:

        return f"HTTP error occurred: {http_err}"

    except Exception as err:

        return f"An error occurred: {err}"
```

Explanation:

- try-except blocks handle errors gracefully.
- If the API call fails, the system won't crash.

Exercise: Build Your Own API Integration

Task:

1. Connect to a **currency exchange API**.
2. Create a tool that converts USD to EUR.

3. Integrate it with LangChain's agent.

Hint: Use <u>ExchangeRate-API</u> or any free currency API.

Connecting LangChain to external APIs and data sources transforms static AI models into dynamic, real-time intelligent systems. With the ability to fetch live data, perform specialized tasks, and interact with the world, your AI applications become significantly more powerful and practical.

2.4 Building a Simple LangChain Workflow

In this section, I'll walk you step-by-step through creating a simple yet practical LangChain workflow. You'll see how to connect different components, manage input and output, and build a system that responds intelligently to user input. This hands-on example will provide the foundation you need to start creating more complex workflows.

Workflow Objective

Let's build a simple AI-powered assistant that can:

1. Generate product descriptions for an e-commerce site.
2. Perform basic calculations when asked.
3. Provide fallback responses when it can't handle a request.

This small project will introduce you to creating workflows that handle multiple tasks and make intelligent decisions.

Step 1: Setting Up the Environment

Before writing the code, make sure your environment is ready.

Install Dependencies

Run the following command in your terminal:

```
pip install langchain openai python-dotenv
```

- langchain: The core framework.
- openai: To access OpenAI models.
- python-dotenv: For secure API key management.

Configure API Keys

```
Create a .env file in your project directory and
add your OpenAI API key:
```

```
OPENAI_API_KEY=your_openai_api_key
```

```
In your Python script, load the API key:
```

```
from dotenv import load_dotenv
```

```
import os
```

```
load_dotenv()
```

```
openai_api_key = os.getenv("OPENAI_API_KEY")
```

Step 2: Define the Workflow Components

1. Product Description Generator (Prompt + Chain)

We'll start by creating a prompt to generate product descriptions.

```
from langchain import OpenAI, LLMChain
```

```
from langchain.prompts import PromptTemplate
```

```python
# Initialize the language model

llm = OpenAI(temperature=0.7)


# Define a prompt template for product
descriptions

product_prompt = PromptTemplate(

    input_variables=["product"],

    template="Write an engaging product
description for {product}."

)


# Create a chain for product description
generation

product_chain = LLMChain(llm=llm,
prompt=product_prompt)
```

Explanation:

- The prompt defines how the model should generate the description.
- The chain connects the prompt to the model, forming a reusable workflow.

2. Calculator Tool

Now, let's create a tool to handle basic math calculations.

```python
from langchain.utilities import PythonREPL
```

```
# Initialize Python REPL as a calculator tool

calculator_tool = PythonREPL()
```

Explanation:
The Python REPL tool lets the AI evaluate math expressions. It's perfect for handling basic calculations.

3. Default Response for Unsupported Queries

If the assistant can't handle a request, it should respond gracefully.

```
def default_response(query):

    return "I'm sorry, I can't help with that
request right now."
```

Explanation:
This function acts as a safety net for unsupported inputs, improving the user experience.

Step 3: Creating the Decision Logic

Now, let's combine these components into a decision-making workflow. The assistant will:

- Generate product descriptions when the user asks for them.
- Solve math problems when it detects calculations.
- Provide a fallback response when it doesn't understand the input.

Complete Workflow Code

```
import re

# Decision-making workflow
```

```python
def assistant_workflow(user_input):

    # Check for product description request

    if "describe" in user_input.lower():

        product =
user_input.lower().replace("describe",
"").strip()

        return product_chain.run(product)


    # Check for math calculation using a simple
pattern

    elif re.search(r'\d+[\+\-\*/]\d+',
user_input):

        return calculator_tool.run(user_input)


    # Default response for unsupported queries

    else:

        return default_response(user_input)


# Test the workflow

print(assistant_workflow("Describe a
smartphone"))

print(assistant_workflow("45 * 3 + 10"))

print(assistant_workflow("Tell me a joke"))
```

Expected Output:

Introducing our latest smartphone: sleek design, cutting-edge technology, and all-day battery life. Perfect for staying connected in style.

145

I'm sorry, I can't help with that request right now.

Explanation:

1. Product Description: When the user asks to "describe," the workflow triggers the product description generator.
2. Math Calculation: If the input looks like a math problem (detected with a regular expression), the calculator tool handles it.
3. Fallback: For anything else, the assistant returns a polite default response.

Step 4: Expanding the Workflow with an Agent

Let's improve this workflow by using a LangChain Agent, which can make decisions more intelligently.

Using an Agent for Dynamic Task Selection

```
from langchain.agents import initialize_agent,
Tool


# Define tools for the agent

tools = [
```

```
    Tool(name="Product Description",
func=product_chain.run, description="Generates
product descriptions."),

    Tool(name="Calculator",
func=calculator_tool.run, description="Performs
math calculations.")

]



# Initialize the agent with the tools

agent = initialize_agent(tools, llm,
agent_type="zero-shot-react-description",
verbose=True)



# Run the agent with different inputs

print(agent.run("Describe wireless headphones"))

print(agent.run("What is 120 / 4?"))

print(agent.run("Tell me a joke"))
```

Expected Output:

Experience the ultimate sound quality with our wireless headphones—designed for comfort, durability, and crystal-clear audio.

30

I'm sorry, I can't help with that request right now.

Explanation:

- The **agent** automatically selects the best tool based on the user input.
- No need for manual logic—the agent figures out whether to generate text or perform a calculation.

Step 5: Handling Errors Gracefully

Let's add error handling to make the assistant more reliable.

```
def safe_assistant_workflow(user_input):

    try:

        return assistant_workflow(user_input)

    except Exception as e:

        return f"An error occurred: {e}"



# Test error handling

print(safe_assistant_workflow("Describe a
smartwatch"))

print(safe_assistant_workflow("10 / 0"))   #
Division by zero
```

Expected Output:

Introducing our latest smartwatch: sleek design with fitness tracking and notifications.

An error occurred: division by zero

Explanation:
This addition makes the assistant more robust by catching errors and responding gracefully.

Exercise: Customize Your Workflow

Task:
Expand this assistant by adding a new tool that:

1. Provides inspirational quotes when the user asks.
2. Uses error handling to manage API failures gracefully.

Hint:

- Use a predefined list of quotes or integrate a quotes API.
- Add the new tool to the agent for dynamic decision-making.

Chapter 3: Mastering LangGraph for Workflow Design

In the previous chapters, we explored how to build linear and dynamic workflows using LangChain. However, as workflows become more complex—especially when they involve branching decisions, looping processes, or error handling—a linear structure is no longer sufficient. This is where LangGraph comes into play. LangGraph offers a more powerful and flexible way to design workflows by representing them as graphs with nodes and edges. This allows for the creation of adaptive, scalable, and intelligent AI systems.

In this chapter, we'll thoroughly explore LangGraph, covering its core concepts and guiding you through creating, managing, and testing adaptive workflows.

3.1 Introduction to LangGraph

LangGraph is a graph-based workflow engine designed to model complex AI workflows in a more natural, flexible, and scalable way. Instead of forcing workflows into a rigid sequence, LangGraph allows you to design adaptable processes using nodes and edges, which represent tasks and transitions. In this section, I'll explain what LangGraph is, why it's essential for building intelligent workflows, and how it helps solve real-world problems that simple workflows cannot.

The Problem with Linear Workflows

Traditional workflows are linear—they follow a strict, step-by-step path. This works for simple tasks but becomes problematic for more dynamic systems.

Challenges with Linear Workflows:

1. Limited Flexibility: Hard to handle branching decisions or unexpected scenarios.
2. Poor Error Handling: Failures in one step can break the entire workflow.
3. No Dynamic Adaptation: Cannot easily change behavior based on user input or system state.
4. Difficult to Scale: As workflows grow, managing them becomes complex and unwieldy.

How LangGraph Solves These Problems

LangGraph solves these challenges by structuring workflows as graphs. A graph is a collection of nodes (tasks) connected by edges (transitions). This design allows workflows to:

- Branch: Adapt based on conditions or inputs.
- Loop: Repeat tasks until a condition is met.
- Parallelize: Run multiple tasks at the same time.
- Recover: Handle errors gracefully and continue processing.

Key Concepts of LangGraph

To fully understand how LangGraph works, we need to look at its core components.

1. Nodes

A Node is a task or decision point in the workflow. It could be a model generating text, a function calling an API, or a condition check.

Examples:

- A chatbot analyzing a user query.
- A system checking if a user is authenticated.
- A model generating a response.

2. Edges

An Edge is the connection between nodes. It defines how the workflow moves from one task to another.

Examples:

- Moving from a user query analysis node to a search API call.
- Transitioning to an error handler if an API fails.

3. Conditions

Edges can have conditions that determine which path to follow based on logic.

Examples:

- If the user asks for a refund, move to the refund processing node.
- If the user asks a general question, proceed to the FAQ answer node.

LangGraph vs. Traditional Workflows

Feature	Traditional Workflow	LangGraph Workflow
Structure	Linear (Step-by-step)	Graph (Nodes and Edges)
Adaptability	Low (Predefined steps)	High (Dynamic and conditional transitions)

Error Handling	Limited (Manual)	Built-in fallback paths
Complexity	Hard to scale for complex tasks	Easily scales with branching and looping
Parallelism	Sequential execution only	Supports parallel execution

Real-World Example: Customer Support Workflow

Let's apply LangGraph to a real-world scenario.

Scenario:

A customer service assistant must handle these cases:

1. FAQs → Answer common questions.
2. Complaints → Escalate to a human agent.
3. Refund Requests → Start the refund process.

Traditional Workflow Limitation:

In a linear workflow, handling these different cases would require complex if-else logic, making the system hard to maintain.

LangGraph Workflow Solution:

In LangGraph, this can be modeled as a graph:

```
[Start] → [Classify Query] → [Answer FAQ]
                            ↘
                    [Escalate Complaint]
                            ↘
                    [Process Refund]
```

Code Example: Basic LangGraph Workflow

```python
from langgraph import Graph, Node


# Define task nodes
def start_node(input_data):

    return "classify_query", input_data


def classify_query(input_data):

    if "refund" in input_data.lower():

        return "process_refund", input_data

    elif "complaint" in input_data.lower():

        return "escalate_complaint", input_data

    else:

        return "answer_faq", input_data
```

```python
def answer_faq(input_data):

    return "Here's the information you
requested."


def escalate_complaint(input_data):

    return "Your complaint has been escalated to
support."


def process_refund(input_data):

    return "Your refund request is being
processed."


# Create the workflow graph

workflow = Graph()

workflow.add_node("start", start_node)

workflow.add_node("classify_query",
classify_query)

workflow.add_node("answer_faq", answer_faq)

workflow.add_node("escalate_complaint",
escalate_complaint)

workflow.add_node("process_refund",
process_refund)
```

```
# Define transitions between nodes

workflow.add_edge("start", "classify_query")

workflow.add_edge("classify_query", "answer_faq",
condition=lambda x: "refund" not in x.lower() and
"complaint" not in x.lower())

workflow.add_edge("classify_query",
"escalate_complaint", condition=lambda x:
"complaint" in x.lower())

workflow.add_edge("classify_query",
"process_refund", condition=lambda x: "refund" in
x.lower())


# Run the workflow

print(workflow.run("I want a refund"))

print(workflow.run("I have a complaint"))

print(workflow.run("What are your store hours?"))
```

Expected Output:

Your refund request is being processed.

Your complaint has been escalated to support.

Here's the information you requested.

Explanation:

- Nodes handle specific tasks (answering FAQs, processing refunds, escalating complaints).

- Edges with conditions decide which path to follow based on the user's input.

Exercise: Extend the Workflow

Objective:
Add a new feature that handles **order tracking** requests.

Steps to Follow:

1. Create a new node called track_order.
2. Update the classifier to detect the word "order."
3. Connect the new node to the workflow.

LangGraph provides a flexible, scalable solution for designing intelligent workflows. By using nodes to represent tasks and edges to define transitions, LangGraph allows you to:

- Adapt to user input dynamically.
- Simplify complex workflows.
- Implement error handling and fallback logic.

3.2 Nodes and Edges

To truly master LangGraph, it's essential to understand its two most fundamental components: Nodes and Edges. These are the backbone of how LangGraph structures and executes workflows. In this section, I'll explain in detail what Nodes and Edges are, how they work together to create dynamic workflows, and provide practical, working code examples to help you understand how to use them effectively.

What Are Nodes in LangGraph?

A Node represents a specific task, function, or decision point in a workflow. It's where the "work" happens—processing input, making decisions, or performing actions. Nodes can be as simple as returning a value or as complex as calling external APIs or executing multiple steps.

Types of Nodes:

1. Action Nodes: Perform specific tasks (e.g., API calls, data processing).
2. Decision Nodes: Analyze input and decide what the next step should be.
3. Error Handling Nodes: Manage failures and define recovery steps.
4. Loop Nodes: Repeat certain actions until a condition is met.

Example: Node for Processing Customer Queries

```
def classify_query(user_input):

    if "refund" in user_input.lower():

        return "process_refund", user_input

    elif "complaint" in user_input.lower():

        return "escalate_complaint", user_input

    else:

        return "handle_faq", user_input
```

Explanation:

- This Decision Node examines the user's input and routes it to the correct next step:
    - Refund requests go to "process_refund".
    - Complaints go to "escalate_complaint".
    - All other queries are handled by "handle_faq".

What Are Edges in LangGraph?

An Edge connects two nodes and defines how the workflow moves from one node to the next. Edges can be unconditional (always proceed) or conditional (proceed only if a certain condition is met).

Types of Edges:

1. Standard Edges: Direct transitions without conditions.
2. Conditional Edges: Transitions based on specific logic or criteria.
3. Fallback Edges: Define alternate paths in case of failure.

Example: Conditional Edge for Decision-Making

```
workflow.add_edge("classify_query",
"process_refund", condition=lambda x: "refund" in
x.lower())

workflow.add_edge("classify_query",
"escalate_complaint", condition=lambda x:
"complaint" in x.lower())

workflow.add_edge("classify_query", "handle_faq",
condition=lambda x: "refund" not in x.lower() and
"complaint" not in x.lower())
```

Explanation:

- If the input contains the word "refund", it transitions to the "process_refund" node.
- If it contains "complaint", it transitions to the "escalate_complaint" node.
- For all other inputs, it transitions to the "handle_faq" node.

Building a Complete Workflow with Nodes and Edges

Let's bring these concepts together and build a fully functional workflow.

Scenario:

A customer service bot needs to:

1. Classify queries as FAQ, complaints, or refund requests.
2. Process refunds when requested.
3. Escalate complaints to a human agent.
4. Answer FAQs for general inquiries.

Step-by-Step Code Example

```python
from langgraph import Graph



# Define Nodes

def start_node(user_input):

    return "classify_query", user_input



def classify_query(user_input):

    if "refund" in user_input.lower():

        return "process_refund", user_input

    elif "complaint" in user_input.lower():

        return "escalate_complaint", user_input

    else:

        return "handle_faq", user_input
```

```python
def process_refund(user_input):

    return "Your refund request has been
received. Processing it now."


def escalate_complaint(user_input):

    return "Your complaint has been escalated to
our support team."


def handle_faq(user_input):

    return "Here is the information you
requested."


# Initialize the workflow graph

workflow = Graph()


# Add Nodes

workflow.add_node("start", start_node)

workflow.add_node("classify_query",
classify_query)

workflow.add_node("process_refund",
process_refund)
```

```
workflow.add_node("escalate_complaint",
escalate_complaint)

workflow.add_node("handle_faq", handle_faq)


# Define Edges

workflow.add_edge("start", "classify_query")

workflow.add_edge("classify_query",
"process_refund", condition=lambda x: "refund" in
x.lower())

workflow.add_edge("classify_query",
"escalate_complaint", condition=lambda x:
"complaint" in x.lower())

workflow.add_edge("classify_query", "handle_faq",
condition=lambda x: "refund" not in x.lower() and
"complaint" not in x.lower())


# Run the workflow with different inputs

print(workflow.run("I want a refund for my
order."))

print(workflow.run("I have a complaint about your
service."))

print(workflow.run("What are your store hours?"))
```

Expected Output:

Your refund request has been received. Processing it now.

Your complaint has been escalated to our support team.

Here is the information you requested.

Explanation:

1. The start_node passes the input to classify_query.
2. classify_query analyzes the input and decides which path to follow.
3. The workflow transitions to the appropriate node based on the input.
4. Edges manage the flow between nodes with clear conditions.

Advanced Node and Edge Usage

1. Looping with Nodes

Let's create a loop where the workflow repeatedly asks for valid input until the user types "exit".

```
def validate_input(user_input):

    if user_input.lower() == "exit":

        return "end", "Goodbye!"

    else:

        return "validate_input", "Invalid input.
Please type 'exit' to quit."



def end_workflow(message):

    return message
```

```python
# Update the graph

workflow.add_node("validate_input",
validate_input)

workflow.add_node("end", end_workflow)


workflow.add_edge("start", "validate_input")

workflow.add_edge("validate_input",
"validate_input", condition=lambda x: x.lower()
!= "exit")

workflow.add_edge("validate_input", "end",
condition=lambda x: x.lower() == "exit")


# Test the loop

print(workflow.run("hello"))

print(workflow.run("exit"))
```

Expected Output:

Invalid input. Please type 'exit' to quit.

Goodbye!

Explanation:

- The workflow loops on the validate_input node until the user types "exit".
- Once "exit" is detected, it transitions to the end node.

Exercise: Build Your Own Workflow

Task:

1. Add a new node called "track_order" that responds when the user asks about order tracking.
2. Update the classifier to detect the word "track".
3. Add a new edge to connect this feature.

Hint:

- Use the existing structure of nodes and edges.
- Define conditions based on user input.

Understanding **Nodes** and **Edges** is critical for designing powerful, adaptive workflows in LangGraph. Nodes allow you to break down complex tasks into smaller, manageable steps, while edges give you full control over how your workflow transitions between tasks.

3.3 Creating Adaptive and Branching Workflows

In real-world applications, workflows rarely follow a simple, linear path. Systems must adapt to user input, handle exceptions, and make decisions dynamically. This is where adaptive and branching workflows come into play. They enable AI systems to be flexible, responsive, and capable of handling complex tasks. In this section, we'll explore how to build adaptive and branching workflows using LangGraph. I'll guide you through the concepts and provide complete, working code examples to ensure you can apply these ideas effectively.

What Are Adaptive and Branching Workflows?

An adaptive workflow can adjust its path based on changing inputs or conditions. A branching workflow introduces decision points where the flow can split into multiple paths depending on logic or user input.

Why Are They Important?

- Dynamic Decision-Making: Responds differently based on user intent or external data.
- Error Recovery: Redirects to backup steps when errors occur.
- Scalability: Handles complex, multi-step tasks efficiently.
- User-Centric Responses: Tailors interactions to user needs.

Real-World Examples:

1. Customer Support Chatbot:
   - Answers FAQs.
   - Processes refund requests.
   - Escalates complaints to human agents.
2. E-commerce Checkout Flow:
   - Offers payment options.
   - Applies discounts if a code is valid.
   - Handles payment failures with retries.

Core Components for Adaptive Workflows

1. Decision Nodes: Evaluate conditions and direct the flow accordingly.

2. Conditional Edges: Define rules for transitioning between tasks based on outcomes.

3. Fallback Paths: Provide alternative routes when errors or unexpected inputs occur.

4. Looping Nodes: Repeat actions until a condition is satisfied.

Building an Adaptive Workflow: A Customer Support Assistant

Scenario:

A customer support assistant must:

1. Answer FAQs for general questions.
2. Process refund requests.
3. Escalate complaints to human agents.
4. Handle invalid inputs gracefully.

Step 1: Define the Nodes

Each task in the workflow will be represented by a **Node**.

```python
from langgraph import Graph
```

```python
# Start node that directs input to the classifier

def start_node(user_input):

    return "classify_query", user_input
```

```python
# Classify the user's input into categories

def classify_query(user_input):

    if "refund" in user_input.lower():

        return "process_refund", user_input

    elif "complaint" in user_input.lower():

        return "escalate_complaint", user_input
```

```python
    elif "help" in user_input.lower() or "faq" in
user_input.lower():

        return "handle_faq", user_input

    else:

        return "handle_invalid_input", user_input


# Respond to FAQs

def handle_faq(user_input):

    return "Here is the answer to your frequently
asked question."


# Process refund requests

def process_refund(user_input):

    return "Your refund request has been
submitted."


# Escalate complaints

def escalate_complaint(user_input):

    return "Your complaint has been escalated to
our support team."


# Handle invalid or unrecognized input
```

```
def handle_invalid_input(user_input):

    return "I'm sorry, I didn't understand your
request. Can you please clarify?"
```

Explanation:

- The start node receives user input.
- Classify Query Node evaluates the input and routes it accordingly.
- Other nodes handle specific tasks.

Step 2: Define the Edges

Now, we'll connect these nodes using **Edges** to define how the workflow moves between tasks.

```
# Initialize the workflow graph

workflow = Graph()



# Add nodes to the workflow

workflow.add_node("start", start_node)

workflow.add_node("classify_query",
classify_query)

workflow.add_node("handle_faq", handle_faq)

workflow.add_node("process_refund",
process_refund)

workflow.add_node("escalate_complaint",
escalate_complaint)
```

```
workflow.add_node("handle_invalid_input",
handle_invalid_input)


# Define edges between nodes

workflow.add_edge("start", "classify_query")

workflow.add_edge("classify_query", "handle_faq",
condition=lambda x: "help" in x.lower() or "faq"
in x.lower())

workflow.add_edge("classify_query",
"process_refund", condition=lambda x: "refund" in
x.lower())

workflow.add_edge("classify_query",
"escalate_complaint", condition=lambda x:
"complaint" in x.lower())

workflow.add_edge("classify_query",
"handle_invalid_input", condition=lambda x:
all(word not in x.lower() for word in ["refund",
"complaint", "help", "faq"]))
```

Explanation:

- Edges direct the flow based on user input.
- Conditions are applied to edges to trigger the correct next node.

Step 3: Running the Workflow

Let's test how this adaptive workflow responds to different user inputs.

```
# Test the workflow with different inputs
```

```
print(workflow.run("I need a refund for my
order."))

print(workflow.run("I have a complaint about the
service."))

print(workflow.run("Can you help me with FAQs?"))

print(workflow.run("Tell me something
interesting."))
```

Expected Output:

Your refund request has been submitted.

Your complaint has been escalated to our support team.

Here is the answer to your frequently asked question.

I'm sorry, I didn't understand your request. Can you please clarify?

Explanation:

- The workflow **adapts** to user input and **branches** accordingly.
- Unrecognized input is handled gracefully.

Advanced Example: Adding Fallbacks and Looping

Let's improve this workflow by handling errors and allowing retries for refund processing.

Step 1: Introduce Error Handling

```
import random

def process_refund(user_input):

    # Simulate a system error 50% of the time
```

```
    if random.choice([True, False]):

        return "refund_error", "Refund system is
currently down."

    else:

        return "refund_success", "Your refund
request has been submitted."


def refund_error_handler(user_input):

    return "We are currently experiencing issues.
Would you like to try again later?"


def refund_success(user_input):

    return user_input  # Pass through success
message
```

Step 2: Update the Graph with Fallbacks

```
# Add new nodes for error handling

workflow.add_node("refund_error",
refund_error_handler)

workflow.add_node("refund_success",
refund_success)


# Define edges for error handling
```

```
workflow.add_edge("process_refund",
"refund_error", condition=lambda x:  "error" in
x.lower())

workflow.add_edge("process_refund",
"refund_success", condition=lambda x:  "submitted"
in x.lower())

workflow.add_edge("refund_error",
"process_refund", condition=lambda x:  "retry" in
x.lower())
```

Explanation:

- The workflow now handles errors and offers a retry option.
- Fallback paths improve resilience.

Step 3: Testing Error Handling

```
print(workflow.run("I need a refund for my
order."))

print(workflow.run("retry"))   # Simulates
retrying the refund process
```

Expected Output (Example):

We are currently experiencing issues. Would you like to try again later?

Your refund request has been submitted.

Exercise: Expand the Workflow

Task:

1. Add a new node called "track_order" to provide order tracking updates.
2. Update the classifier to detect the word "track".

3. Handle errors if the order system is unavailable.

3.3 Creating Adaptive and Branching Workflows

Workflows rarely follow a simple, linear path. Systems must adapt to user input, handle exceptions, and make decisions dynamically. This is where adaptive and branching workflows come into play. They enable AI systems to be flexible, responsive, and capable of handling complex tasks. In this section, we'll explore how to build adaptive and branching workflows using LangGraph. I'll guide you through the concepts and provide complete, working code examples to ensure you can apply these ideas effectively.

What Are Adaptive and Branching Workflows?

An adaptive workflow can adjust its path based on changing inputs or conditions. A branching workflow introduces decision points where the flow can split into multiple paths depending on logic or user input.

Why Are They Important?

- Dynamic Decision-Making: Responds differently based on user intent or external data.
- Error Recovery: Redirects to backup steps when errors occur.
- Scalability: Handles complex, multi-step tasks efficiently.
- User-Centric Responses: Tailors interactions to user needs.

Real-World Examples:

1. **Customer Support Chatbot:**
   - Answers FAQs.
   - Processes refund requests.
   - Escalates complaints to human agents.

2. **E-commerce Checkout Flow:**
   - Offers payment options.
   - Applies discounts if a code is valid.
   - Handles payment failures with retries.

Core Components for Adaptive Workflows

1. Decision Nodes: Evaluate conditions and direct the flow accordingly.

2. Conditional Edges: Define rules for transitioning between tasks based on outcomes.

3. Fallback Paths: Provide alternative routes when errors or unexpected inputs occur.

4. Looping Nodes: Repeat actions until a condition is satisfied.

Building an Adaptive Workflow: A Customer Support Assistant

Scenario:

A customer support assistant must:

1. Answer FAQs for general questions.
2. Process refund requests.
3. Escalate complaints to human agents.
4. Handle invalid inputs gracefully.

Step 1: Define the Nodes

Each task in the workflow will be represented by a Node.

```
from langgraph import Graph
```

```python
# Start node that directs input to the classifier
def start_node(user_input):

    return "classify_query", user_input


# Classify the user's input into categories
def classify_query(user_input):

    if "refund" in user_input.lower():

        return "process_refund", user_input

    elif "complaint" in user_input.lower():

        return "escalate_complaint", user_input

    elif "help" in user_input.lower() or "faq" in
user_input.lower():

        return "handle_faq", user_input

    else:

        return "handle_invalid_input", user_input


# Respond to FAQs
def handle_faq(user_input):

    return "Here is the answer to your frequently
asked question."
```

```
# Process refund requests

def process_refund(user_input):

    return "Your refund request has been
submitted."
```

```
# Escalate complaints

def escalate_complaint(user_input):

    return "Your complaint has been escalated to
our support team."
```

```
# Handle invalid or unrecognized input

def handle_invalid_input(user_input):

    return "I'm sorry, I didn't understand your
request. Can you please clarify?"
```

Explanation:

- The start node receives user input.
- Classify Query Node evaluates the input and routes it accordingly.
- Other nodes handle specific tasks.

Step 2: Define the Edges

Now, we'll connect these nodes using **Edges** to define how the workflow moves between tasks.

```
# Initialize the workflow graph
```

```python
workflow = Graph()


# Add nodes to the workflow

workflow.add_node("start", start_node)

workflow.add_node("classify_query",
classify_query)

workflow.add_node("handle_faq", handle_faq)

workflow.add_node("process_refund",
process_refund)

workflow.add_node("escalate_complaint",
escalate_complaint)

workflow.add_node("handle_invalid_input",
handle_invalid_input)


# Define edges between nodes

workflow.add_edge("start", "classify_query")

workflow.add_edge("classify_query", "handle_faq",
condition=lambda x: "help" in x.lower() or "faq"
in x.lower())

workflow.add_edge("classify_query",
"process_refund", condition=lambda x: "refund" in
x.lower())

workflow.add_edge("classify_query",
"escalate_complaint", condition=lambda x:
"complaint" in x.lower())
```

```
workflow.add_edge("classify_query",
"handle_invalid_input", condition=lambda x:
all(word not in x.lower() for word in ["refund",
"complaint", "help", "faq"]))
```

Explanation:

- **Edges** direct the flow based on user input.
- Conditions are applied to edges to trigger the correct next node.

Step 3: Running the Workflow

Let's test how this adaptive workflow responds to different user inputs.

```
# Test the workflow with different inputs

print(workflow.run("I need a refund for my
order."))

print(workflow.run("I have a complaint about the
service."))

print(workflow.run("Can you help me with FAQs?"))

print(workflow.run("Tell me something
interesting."))
```

Expected Output:

Your refund request has been submitted.

Your complaint has been escalated to our support team.

Here is the answer to your frequently asked question.

I'm sorry, I didn't understand your request. Can you please clarify?

Explanation:

- The workflow adapts to user input and branches accordingly.
- Unrecognized input is handled gracefully.

Advanced Example: Adding Fallbacks and Looping

Let's improve this workflow by handling errors and allowing retries for refund processing.

Step 1: Introduce Error Handling

```python
import random


def process_refund(user_input):

    # Simulate a system error 50% of the time

    if random.choice([True, False]):

        return "refund_error", "Refund system is currently down."

    else:

        return "refund_success", "Your refund request has been submitted."


def refund_error_handler(user_input):

    return "We are currently experiencing issues. Would you like to try again later?"
```

```
def refund_success(user_input):

    return user_input  # Pass through success
message
```

Step 2: Update the Graph with Fallbacks

```
# Add new nodes for error handling

workflow.add_node("refund_error",
refund_error_handler)

workflow.add_node("refund_success",
refund_success)
```

```
# Define edges for error handling

workflow.add_edge("process_refund",
"refund_error", condition=lambda x: "error" in
x.lower())

workflow.add_edge("process_refund",
"refund_success", condition=lambda x: "submitted"
in x.lower())

workflow.add_edge("refund_error",
"process_refund", condition=lambda x: "retry" in
x.lower())
```

Explanation:

- The workflow now handles errors and offers a retry option.
- Fallback paths improve resilience.

Step 3: Testing Error Handling

```
print(workflow.run("I need a refund for my
order."))

print(workflow.run("retry"))  # Simulates
retrying the refund process
```

Expected Output (Example):

We are currently experiencing issues. Would you like to try again later?

Your refund request has been submitted.

Exercise: Expand the Workflow

Task:

1. Add a new node called "track_order" to provide order tracking updates.
2. Update the classifier to detect the word "track".
3. Handle errors if the order system is unavailable.

3.5 Debugging and Testing LangGraph Workflows

Building complex, adaptive workflows with LangGraph is a powerful way to create dynamic AI systems. However, as workflows grow in complexity, debugging and testing become critical. Without proper debugging and testing, even well-designed workflows can break, produce incorrect results, or fail silently. In this section, I'll guide you through effective strategies to debug and test LangGraph workflows. You'll learn practical methods to identify and fix issues, ensure reliability, and maintain the performance of your workflows.

Why Debugging and Testing Matter

- Identify Errors Early: Catch issues before they affect users.
- Ensure Workflow Accuracy: Validate that workflows perform as expected.
- Improve Stability: Handle edge cases and unexpected input gracefully.
- Simplify Maintenance: Easier to update workflows when they are well-tested.

Common Workflow Issues

Before we get into debugging and testing, it's important to recognize common issues in LangGraph workflows:

1. Incorrect Node Logic: A node performs the wrong task or produces incorrect output.
2. Broken Transitions: Edges don't correctly move between nodes.
3. Uncaught Errors: Failures in external API calls or tools that aren't handled.
4. Infinite Loops: The workflow gets stuck looping due to poor exit conditions.
5. State Mismanagement: Workflow state isn't updated or shared correctly between nodes.

Debugging LangGraph Workflows

1. Adding Debugging Logs

Logging is one of the simplest and most effective ways to understand what your workflow is doing. It helps you trace how data moves between nodes and where things might be breaking.

Code Example: Adding Logs to Nodes

```
def classify_query(user_input):
```

```python
    print(f"[DEBUG] Classifying input:
{user_input}")  # Debug log

    if "refund" in user_input.lower():

        print("[DEBUG] Routing to
'process_refund' node.")

        return "process_refund", user_input

    elif "complaint" in user_input.lower():

        print("[DEBUG] Routing to
'escalate_complaint' node.")

        return "escalate_complaint", user_input

    else:

        print("[DEBUG] Routing to 'handle_faq'
node.")

        return "handle_faq", user_input
```

Explanation:

- Debug Logs print the input and decision path.
- If the workflow takes an unexpected path, these logs reveal where it went wrong.

2. Tracking Node Transitions

LangGraph doesn't log transitions between nodes by default, so adding logs at the transition points can help.

Code Example: Tracking Transitions

```python
def log_transition(from_node, to_node, data):
```

```
    print(f"[TRANSITION] Moving from
'{from_node}' to '{to_node}' with data: {data}")
```

Usage in Workflow:

```
workflow.add_edge("classify_query",
"process_refund",

                condition=lambda x: "refund" in
x.lower(),

                action=lambda x:
log_transition("classify_query",
"process_refund", x))
```

Explanation:
 This logs the transition between nodes, showing what data is moving through the workflow.

3. Handling and Logging Errors

Failures in API calls or external tools can break workflows. Adding **try-except blocks inside nodes** helps catch and log these errors.

Code Example: Error Logging

```
def process_refund(user_input):

    try:

        # Simulating an API call that may fail

        if "fail" in user_input:

            raise ValueError("Simulated API
failure.")

        return "Your refund has been processed."
```

```
except Exception as e:

        print(f"[ERROR] Failed to process refund:
{e}")

        return "refund_error", "There was a
problem processing your refund."
```

Explanation:

- Catches any unexpected errors during refund processing.
- Logs the error and redirects to an error-handling node.

Testing LangGraph Workflows

Testing verifies that workflows operate as intended. LangGraph workflows should be tested with different inputs, edge cases, and simulated errors.

1. Manual Testing

Start by manually running the workflow with various inputs to check behavior.

Code Example: Manual Testing

```
print(workflow.run("I need a refund."))

print(workflow.run("I have a complaint."))

print(workflow.run("Tell me about your
products."))

print(workflow.run("fail refund"))
```

Expected Output:

Your refund has been processed.

Your complaint has been escalated.

Here is the answer to your question.

There was a problem processing your refund.

2. Automated Testing

For larger workflows, automated testing is essential. You can use Python's unittest framework to automate the process.

Code Example: Automated Testing with unittest

```
import unittest


class
TestCustomerSupportWorkflow(unittest.TestCase):


    def test_refund_request(self):

        result = workflow.run("I need a refund.")

        self.assertEqual(result, "Your refund has
been processed.")


    def test_complaint_handling(self):

        result = workflow.run("I have a
complaint.")

        self.assertEqual(result, "Your complaint
has been escalated.")
```

```python
    def test_invalid_input(self):

        result = workflow.run("Tell me something random.")

        self.assertEqual(result, "Here is the answer to your question.")


    def test_refund_error(self):

        result = workflow.run("fail refund")

        self.assertEqual(result, "There was a problem processing your refund.")


if __name__ == '__main__':

    unittest.main()
```

Explanation:

- Automated tests check that each workflow path behaves correctly.
- Errors like broken transitions or incorrect responses are caught early.

3. Testing Edge Cases

Edge cases often cause unexpected failures. Testing for these ensures the workflow is robust.

Examples of Edge Cases to Test:

- Empty Input: ""
- Unexpected Input: "random gibberish"
- Multiple Keywords: "I need a refund and I have a complaint."
- Case Sensitivity: "Refund" vs. "refund"

Code Example: Edge Case Testing

```
def test_empty_input():

    result = workflow.run("")

    assert result == "I'm sorry, I didn't
understand your request."



def test_multiple_keywords():

    result = workflow.run("I need a refund and I
have a complaint.")

    assert result == "Your refund has been
processed."  # Or prioritize complaint handling
```

Explanation:
These tests ensure the workflow can handle unexpected or complex input gracefully.

Exercise: Debugging Practice

Task:

1. Introduce an intentional error in the "escalate_complaint" node (e.g., simulate a failed API call).
2. Add error handling to log the issue and redirect to an "error_handler" node.

3. Write automated tests to verify that the error is handled correctly.

Best Practices for Debugging and Testing

1. Log Critical Transitions: Log data movement between nodes for traceability.
2. Handle Errors Gracefully: Always use try-except blocks for risky operations.
3. Test for Edge Cases: Validate behavior under unexpected conditions.
4. Automate Tests: Use unittest or similar frameworks to automate regression testing.
5. Use Assertions: Assert expected outcomes to catch unexpected behavior.

Chapter 4: Designing Intelligent AI Agents

Building intelligent AI systems requires more than just powerful models—it requires designing **AI agents** that can think, decide, act, and adapt. These agents must handle diverse tasks, make decisions autonomously, and collaborate with other agents or tools. In this chapter, we'll explore how to design intelligent AI agents using modern frameworks like LangChain and LangGraph, focusing on their architectures, communication strategies, decision-making, context management, and error handling.

4.1 Architectures of AI Agents

AI agents are software entities designed to perceive their environment, make decisions, and perform actions to achieve specific goals. The architecture of an AI agent defines how it processes information, responds to changes, and interacts with users or other systems. Choosing the right architecture is critical because it determines the agent's capabilities and behavior in different scenarios. In this section, we will thoroughly discuss the three foundational architectures of AI agents: Reactive, Proactive, and Hybrid. Each architecture serves a unique purpose, and understanding their strengths and limitations will help you design intelligent agents that solve real-world problems effectively.

1. Reactive AI Agents

A Reactive Agent operates solely based on its current inputs from the environment. It responds to stimuli without maintaining memory or context from previous interactions. These agents are rule-driven and lack the ability to plan or adapt beyond predefined behaviors.

Characteristics:

- No memory of past interactions.
- Rule-based responses to specific inputs.
- Immediate and straightforward decision-making.
- Efficient but inflexible for complex tasks.

Real-World Examples:

- Thermostats: Turns heating on/off based on the current temperature.
- Motion-Sensor Lights: Lights turn on when motion is detected and off after a set time.
- Spam Filters: Detects and blocks spam emails based on simple keyword rules.

Advantages:

- Fast response time.
- Low computational cost.
- Simple to design and deploy.

Limitations:

- Cannot handle complex, multi-step tasks.
- No ability to adapt or learn.
- Limited to predefined scenarios.

Code Example: Simple Reactive Agent

Let's create a basic reactive agent that responds to greetings and farewells.

```
def reactive_agent(user_input):

    if "hello" in user_input.lower():

        return "Hi there! How can I assist you?"
```

```
    elif "bye" in user_input.lower():

        return "Goodbye! Have a great day!"

    else:

        return "I'm sorry, I don't understand."


# Testing the reactive agent

print(reactive_agent("Hello"))    # Output: Hi
there! How can I assist you?

print(reactive_agent("Bye"))      # Output:
Goodbye! Have a great day!

print(reactive_agent("What's up?"))   # Output:
I'm sorry, I don't understand.
```

Explanation:

This agent reacts only to the current input. It has no memory of past conversations and cannot adapt to new or unexpected inputs.

2. Proactive AI Agents

A Proactive Agent anticipates future needs and takes the initiative to act without being explicitly prompted. These agents use internal goals and context to decide when and how to take action, even without external triggers.

Characteristics:

- Goal-driven and self-initiating.
- Predicts future needs based on patterns.
- May operate autonomously without user input.
- Can handle planned tasks and scheduled actions.

Real-World Examples:

- Smart Calendar Assistants: Remind users of meetings and suggest leaving early based on traffic.
- Home Automation Systems: Adjust lighting and temperature automatically based on daily routines.
- Predictive Maintenance Systems: Identify potential equipment failures before they happen.

Advantages:

- Improves user experience by anticipating needs.
- Increases efficiency by automating repetitive tasks.
- Can adapt to changing environments over time.

Limitations:

- Higher computational and design complexity.
- Risk of being overly intrusive or annoying if not designed carefully.
- Requires access to data for accurate predictions.

Code Example: Proactive Reminder Agent

Let's build a proactive agent that reminds the user about an upcoming meeting.

```
import datetime
```

```
def proactive_agent():

    current_time = datetime.datetime.now()

    meeting_time =
datetime.datetime(current_time.year,
```

```
current_time.month, current_time.day, 10, 0)  #
10 AM Meeting


    if current_time.hour == 9:

        return "Reminder: You have a meeting at
10 AM. Would you like to prepare?"

    elif current_time >= meeting_time:

        return "Your meeting has started!"

    else:

        return "No reminders at this time."



# Simulate the proactive agent's behavior

print(proactive_agent())
```

Explanation:
This agent checks the current time and proactively reminds the user of their upcoming meeting without being prompted.

3. Hybrid AI Agents

A Hybrid Agent combines both reactive and proactive behaviors. It can respond to immediate inputs while also anticipating and initiating actions based on goals or context. Hybrid agents balance responsiveness with autonomy, making them ideal for complex and dynamic environments.

Characteristics:

- Flexible behavior: reacts when necessary and acts independently when needed.
- Maintains short-term memory and adapts over time.
- Handles multi-step workflows and long-term goals.
- Can collaborate with other agents or tools.

Real-World Examples:

- Virtual Assistants (Siri, Alexa): Respond to direct commands and also provide proactive suggestions.
- Autonomous Vehicles: React to obstacles in real-time while planning routes.
- Smart Home Systems: Adjust lighting based on user activity but also respond to direct voice commands.

Advantages:

- Balanced adaptability: Reacts immediately and plans ahead.
- Context-aware decision-making.
- Handles complexity with more efficiency.

Limitations:

- Higher design complexity than reactive or proactive agents alone.
- Requires careful balance to avoid confusing or overwhelming users.

Code Example: Hybrid Agent

Let's build a hybrid agent that can both answer questions and provide proactive reminders.

```
import datetime
```

```
def hybrid_agent(user_input=None):
```

```python
    current_time = datetime.datetime.now()

    # Proactive behavior

    if current_time.hour == 9 and not user_input:

        return "Good morning! Remember your 10 AM meeting."


    # Reactive behavior

    if user_input:

        if "weather" in user_input.lower():

            return "Today's weather is sunny with a high of 25°C."

        elif "news" in user_input.lower():

            return "Here are today's top headlines..."

        else:

            return "I'm here to help with anything you need."


    return "No updates at the moment."


# Testing proactive and reactive behaviors

print(hybrid_agent())  # Proactive reminder
```

```
print(hybrid_agent("Tell me the weather"))   #
Reactive response
```

Explanation:

- Proactive Behavior: Reminds the user about a meeting if the time is 9 AM.
- Reactive Behavior: Responds to user queries when prompted.

Choosing the Right Agent Architecture

Feature	Reactive Agent	Proactive Agent	Hybrid Agent
Response to Input	Instant reaction	Anticipates actions	Both reactive and proactive
Memory/Context	None	Maintains goals/context	Partial or full context
Complexity	Low	High	Moderate to high
Ideal Use Case	Simple, repetitive tasks	Scheduled/planned tasks	Complex, multi-step systems

| **Examples** | Spam filter, thermostat | Smart assistant reminders | Virtual assistants, robots |

Exercise: Build a Custom Hybrid Agent

Task:

1. Design a hybrid agent that:
    - ○ Responds to greetings and questions.
    - ○ Reminds the user to drink water every hour.
2. Add error handling for unrecognized inputs.

4.2 Multi-Agent Collaboration and Communication

As AI systems become more complex, a single agent handling all tasks is no longer practical. Modern applications require specialized agents working together to solve complex problems, adapt to changing environments, and deliver efficient solutions. This leads us to the concept of multi-agent collaboration and communication. In this section, we will explore how multiple AI agents can cooperate, coordinate, and communicate to achieve complex objectives. You'll learn about the structures that support multi-agent systems, how to implement them, and how they can be used to solve real-world problems effectively.

Why Multi-Agent Collaboration Matters

1. Division of Labor

Complex problems can be broken down into smaller, specialized tasks. Different agents can focus on specific roles, making the system more efficient and easier to scale.

2. Scalability and Flexibility

Adding more agents to handle increasing workloads or new tasks becomes easier than scaling a monolithic system.

3. Fault Tolerance and Redundancy

If one agent fails, others can continue to function, ensuring system reliability.

4. Distributed Intelligence

Agents can operate in parallel and in different environments, processing information locally and sharing results when needed.

Key Components of Multi-Agent Systems

1. Individual Agents: Specialized in specific tasks or decision-making.
2. Communication Protocols: The rules and methods agents use to share information.
3. Coordination Mechanisms: How agents manage dependencies, conflicts, and task assignments.
4. Collaboration Models: Strategies for working together towards common or individual goals.

Types of Multi-Agent Collaboration

1. Cooperative Agents: Agents share a common goal and work together to achieve it.

Example: In a warehouse, one agent manages inventory while another handles delivery schedules.

2. Competitive Agents: Agents work independently, sometimes with conflicting goals.

Example: In online auctions, bidding agents compete to win items.

3. Collaborative Agents: Agents have different goals but must collaborate to achieve mutual benefits.

Example: In a ride-sharing app, a pricing agent collaborates with a demand forecasting agent to balance prices and availability.

Real-World Example: E-commerce Platform

Let's consider an e-commerce system where multiple agents collaborate:

1. Recommendation Agent: Suggests products to customers.
2. Inventory Agent: Checks stock levels.
3. Pricing Agent: Adjusts product prices based on demand.
4. Shipping Agent: Calculates delivery options and timelines.

How They Collaborate:

- The Recommendation Agent suggests a product.
- The Inventory Agent checks if the product is available.
- The Pricing Agent adjusts the price based on stock levels.
- The Shipping Agent provides delivery options.

Building a Multi-Agent System in Python

Let's build a simple collaborative system with three agents:

1. Recommendation Agent
2. Inventory Agent
3. Shipping Agent

Step 1: Define Each Agent

```python
# Recommendation Agent

def recommendation_agent(user_input):

    if "recommend" in user_input.lower():

        return "I recommend the new wireless headphones."

    return None


# Inventory Agent

def inventory_agent(product):

    stock = {"wireless headphones": 15, "smartwatch": 0}

    if stock.get(product, 0) > 0:

        return f"The {product} is in stock."

    else:

        return f"Sorry, the {product} is out of stock."


# Shipping Agent

def shipping_agent(product):

    if product == "wireless headphones":

        return "Free two-day shipping is available."
```

```
        else:

                return "Standard shipping applies."
```

Step 2: Define the Collaboration Logic

```
def multi_agent_system(user_input):

        recommendation =
recommendation_agent(user_input)


        if recommendation:

                product = "wireless headphones"  #
Inferred from the recommendation

                stock_status = inventory_agent(product)

                shipping_info = shipping_agent(product)

                return
f"{recommendation}\n{stock_status}\n{shipping_inf
o}"


        return "How can I assist you today?"


# Testing the system

print(multi_agent_system("Can you recommend
something?"))
```

Expected Output:

I recommend the new wireless headphones.

The wireless headphones are in stock.

Free two-day shipping is available.

Explanation:

- Recommendation Agent suggests a product.
- Inventory Agent checks availability.
- Shipping Agent adds delivery options.
- All agents work together to provide a cohesive response.

Communication Strategies Between Agents

For agents to collaborate effectively, they need reliable ways to communicate. Let's discuss common strategies:

1. Direct Communication: Agents send messages directly to each other. This is simple and fast but can become messy in large systems.

Example:
 The Recommendation Agent directly asks the Inventory Agent if an item is in stock.

2. Shared Data Stores: Agents read from and write to a common database or memory. This decouples agents but requires data consistency management.

Example:
 All agents update and check a shared inventory database.

3. Message Brokers (Pub/Sub Model): Agents publish messages to a broker (like RabbitMQ or Kafka), and other agents subscribe to relevant topics.

Example:
   The Pricing Agent publishes price changes, and the Recommendation Agent updates its suggestions.

Coordination and Conflict Resolution

When multiple agents work together, conflicts can arise. Here's how to manage them:

1. Priority Rules: Assign priorities to agents. Higher-priority agents can override others.

Example:
   A Security Agent might override a User Preference Agent for safety reasons.

2. Voting Mechanism: Agents vote on decisions, and the majority rules.

Example:
   If three pricing models suggest different prices, the system adopts the majority opinion.

3. Arbitration: A dedicated Coordinator Agent resolves conflicts.

Example:
   A Task Manager Agent assigns tasks based on agent availability.

Advanced Example: Adding a Pricing Agent

Let's extend our system by adding a **Pricing Agent** that adjusts the price based on stock levels.

Pricing Agent

```
def pricing_agent(product):

    stock = {"wireless headphones": 15}
```

```python
    base_price = 100


    if stock.get(product, 0) < 5:

        return f"The price for {product} is
${base_price + 20} due to low stock."

    else:

        return f"The price for {product} is
${base_price}."
```

Update Collaboration Logic

```python
def extended_multi_agent_system(user_input):

    recommendation =
recommendation_agent(user_input)


    if recommendation:

        product = "wireless headphones"

        stock_status = inventory_agent(product)

        price_info = pricing_agent(product)

        shipping_info = shipping_agent(product)

        return
f"{recommendation}\n{stock_status}\n{price_info}\
n{shipping_info}"
```

```
        return "How can I assist you today?"
```

```
print(extended_multi_agent_system("Can you
recommend something?"))
```

Expected Output:

I recommend the new wireless headphones.

The wireless headphones are in stock.

The price for wireless headphones is $100.

Free two-day shipping is available.

Exercise: Build Your Own Multi-Agent System

Task:

1. Add a Discount Agent that applies a discount if the user has a promo code.
2. Ensure the Pricing Agent and Discount Agent coordinate to apply the correct price.
3. Implement error handling if a product is out of stock.

Multi-agent collaboration allows AI systems to handle complex tasks efficiently by breaking them into smaller, specialized components. By enabling agents to **communicate** and **coordinate**, we create systems that are more adaptable, scalable, and robust.

4.3 Implementing Dynamic Decision-Making Logic

In today's AI-driven applications, static and pre-programmed decision-making is no longer sufficient. Users expect systems that can adapt, respond intelligently, and make autonomous decisions based on real-time information. This is where dynamic decision-making logic becomes essential. In this section, we will explore how to design and implement dynamic decision-making logic in AI agents. You'll learn how to make agents flexible and intelligent, capable of evaluating situations and selecting the best actions based on input, context, and evolving conditions. I will provide clear, complete code examples and real-world scenarios to solidify your understanding.

What Is Dynamic Decision-Making?

Dynamic decision-making allows an AI agent to choose between multiple actions based on changing conditions or input. Unlike static systems that follow fixed rules, dynamic agents assess situations in real time and make decisions accordingly.

Key Features of Dynamic Decision-Making:

1. Adaptability: Responds to new data or unexpected conditions.
2. Context Awareness: Considers past interactions or environmental factors.
3. Autonomy: Makes decisions without constant human input.
4. Optimization: Chooses the most efficient or beneficial action.

Real-World Examples:

- Smart Assistants: Deciding whether to answer a question or suggest a follow-up action.

- Autonomous Vehicles: Choosing when to accelerate, brake, or change lanes.
- E-commerce Systems: Adjusting pricing based on demand and stock availability.

Approaches to Dynamic Decision-Making

Dynamic decision-making can be implemented in various ways depending on the system's complexity and requirements.

1. Rule-Based Dynamic Decision Making

Uses structured conditions (if-else statements) to handle simple, predictable decisions. This is the simplest form of decision-making logic. It's useful when the conditions are well-known and the outcomes are predictable.

Code Example: Rule-Based Chatbot

```python
def rule_based_agent(user_input):

    if "refund" in user_input.lower():

        return "Sure, I can help with your refund. Please provide your order number."

    elif "complaint" in user_input.lower():

        return "I'm sorry to hear that. Would you like to speak with a support agent?"

    elif "recommend" in user_input.lower():

        return "I recommend our latest wireless headphones."

    else:
```

```
        return "I'm here to help with anything
you need."


# Test the agent

print(rule_based_agent("I need a refund."))

print(rule_based_agent("I have a complaint."))

print(rule_based_agent("Can you recommend
something?"))
```

Expected Output:

Sure, I can help with your refund. Please provide your order number.

I'm sorry to hear that. Would you like to speak with a support agent?

I recommend our latest wireless headphones.

Explanation:
This agent uses direct condition checks to decide the next action. While simple, it lacks adaptability for complex tasks.

2. Utility-Based Decision Making

In utility-based decision-making, the agent assigns a score or "utility" to each action and selects the one with the highest value.

Real-World Example:

A delivery app might choose between a bike, car, or scooter based on traffic and delivery distance.

Code Example: Delivery Mode Selection

```python
def delivery_agent(distance, traffic_level):

    utilities = {

        "bike": 10 if traffic_level == "high" and
distance < 5 else 5,

        "car": 8 if traffic_level == "low" and
distance > 5 else 3,

        "scooter": 6

    }

    # Select the transport mode with the highest
utility

    best_option = max(utilities,
key=utilities.get)

    return f"The best delivery option is:
{best_option}."


# Test the decision-making logic

print(delivery_agent(3, "high"))   # Output: The
best delivery option is: bike.

print(delivery_agent(10, "low"))   # Output: The
best delivery option is: car.
```

Explanation:
The agent evaluates the environment (distance and traffic) and chooses the most efficient transport option based on assigned utilities.

3. Machine Learning-Based Decision Making

Machine learning models can handle complex, dynamic decision-making tasks that are too intricate for rules or utilities alone.

Real-World Example:

A fraud detection system that predicts whether a transaction is fraudulent based on historical data.

Code Example: ML-Based Decision Making

Let's simulate this with a decision tree classifier using sklearn.

```
from sklearn.tree import DecisionTreeClassifier
```

```
# Sample data: [transaction_amount,
transaction_time (hour)]

X = [[100, 14], [5000, 2], [150, 10], [7000, 1]]
# Features

y = [0, 1, 0, 1]  # Labels: 0 = legitimate, 1 =
fraudulent
```

```
# Train the model

model = DecisionTreeClassifier()

model.fit(X, y)
```

```
# New transaction: $6000 at 3 AM

new_transaction = [[6000, 3]]
```

```
prediction = model.predict(new_transaction)
```

```
print("Fraudulent Transaction" if prediction[0]
== 1 else "Legitimate Transaction")
```

Expected Output:

Fraudulent Transaction

Explanation:
 The model predicts fraudulent behavior based on transaction patterns, adapting to complex data without explicit rules.

4. Agent-Based Decision Making with LangChain

LangChain allows agents to make decisions dynamically by integrating multiple tools and models.

Code Example: Intelligent Assistant with LangChain

```
from langchain import OpenAI, LLMChain

from longchain.prompts import PromptTemplate

from langchain.agents import initialize_agent,
Tool


# Initialize the model

llm = OpenAI(temperature=0.7)


# Define a prompt for recommendations
```

```python
recommendation_prompt = PromptTemplate(

    input_variables=["product_type"],

    template="Recommend a {product_type} to a
customer."

)


# Create a chain for recommendations

recommendation_chain = LLMChain(llm=llm,
prompt=recommendation_prompt)


# Define a tool for product recommendations

recommendation_tool = Tool(

    name="Product Recommendation",

    func=recommendation_chain.run,

    description="Suggests products based on
customer needs."

)


# Initialize the agent with the recommendation
tool

agent = initialize_agent([recommendation_tool],
llm, agent_type="zero-shot-react-description")
```

```
# Run the agent

print(agent.run("I need a new smartphone."))
```

Explanation:

- The agent dynamically chooses to run the recommendation tool when the user asks for product suggestions.
- LangChain simplifies connecting decision logic with models and tools.

Best Practices for Dynamic Decision-Making

1. Start Simple, Scale Gradually: Begin with rule-based logic, then add utilities or learning models as complexity grows.
2. Incorporate Context: Use state management to make context-aware decisions.
3. Prioritize Explainability: Ensure the decision-making process is transparent, especially in sensitive applications.
4. Balance Efficiency and Complexity: Choose the simplest decision-making model that meets your needs.
5. Include Fail-Safes: Implement fallback options when the decision logic fails.

Exercise: Build a Multi-Strategy Decision Agent

Task:

1. Create an agent that:
   - Uses rule-based logic for FAQs.
   - Applies utility-based logic for selecting delivery options.
   - Leverages a mock ML model for predicting product returns.
2. Ensure smooth integration between strategies.

Dynamic decision-making transforms AI agents from basic responders into intelligent, autonomous systems capable of adapting to real-world complexity. By leveraging rule-based, utility-based, machine learning-based, and agent-based decision-making models, you can build systems that are flexible, responsive, and capable of making smart decisions.

4.4 Context Awareness and State Management

Context awareness allows an AI agent to understand and remember relevant information from ongoing interactions, the user's environment, or previous interactions. This capability makes interactions more personalized, coherent, and intelligent.

Key Elements of Context Awareness:

1. User Information: Remembering user preferences, past queries, or behavior patterns.
2. Interaction History: Keeping track of previous dialogue turns or actions.
3. Environment State: Adapting to external conditions (time, location, device status).
4. Task Progress: Tracking multi-step tasks or workflows.

Real-World Examples:

- Virtual Assistants (e.g., Alexa, Siri): Remember past commands to suggest relevant actions.
- E-commerce Chatbots: Recall previous shopping preferences for personalized recommendations.
- Navigation Systems: Adapt routes based on traffic data and user preferences.

What is State Management?

State management involves tracking and updating the current status of a system, conversation, or task. It enables AI agents to maintain continuity and manage complex workflows.

Key Components of State Management:

1. Session State: Tracks data relevant to a single user session.
2. Global State: Stores data shared across sessions or users (e.g., system configurations).
3. Persistent State: Saves long-term data across multiple interactions (e.g., user profiles).

Real-World Examples:

- Customer Support Bots: Track if a customer has already provided an order number.
- Gaming AI: Stores the player's progress and achievements.
- Recommendation Systems: Remember previous interactions to refine suggestions.

While **context** is about understanding *what's happening now* and *what has happened before*, **state management** is about *organizing and updating* that information effectively.

- Context Awareness answers *"What should the AI know right now?"*
- State Management answers *"How is that information stored, updated, and accessed?"*

Both are critical for creating agents that feel intelligent and engaging.

Implementing Context Awareness and State Management

1. Simple Context Management Using Variables

For small, single-session workflows, Python dictionaries or variables can store context.

Example: A chatbot that remembers the user's name.

```python
def simple_context_agent(user_input, context={}):

    if "my name is" in user_input.lower():

        name = user_input.split("is")[-1].strip()

        context['name'] = name

        return f"Nice to meet you, {name}!"


    elif "what's my name" in user_input.lower():

        return f"Your name is
{context.get('name', 'I don't know yet.')}"


    return "How can I assist you?"


# Testing the agent

print(simple_context_agent("My name is John"))

print(simple_context_agent("What's my name?"))
```

Expected Output:

Nice to meet you, John!

Your name is John.

Explanation:

The agent remembers the user's name using a simple context dictionary, demonstrating basic state tracking

2. Context and State Management with LangChain

For more sophisticated applications, LangChain offers built-in memory modules to manage state.

Using ConversationBufferMemory to manage dialogue history.

```python
from langchain import OpenAI, ConversationChain

from langchain.memory import
ConversationBufferMemory


# Initialize the model and memory

llm = OpenAI(temperature=0.7)

memory = ConversationBufferMemory()


# Create a conversation chain with memory

conversation = ConversationChain(llm=llm,
memory=memory)


# Simulate conversation

print(conversation.run("Hello, my name is
Alice."))

print(conversation.run("What's my name?"))
```

Expected Output:

Hello Alice! How can I help you today?

Your name is Alice.

Explanation:

- The agent uses LangChain's ConversationBufferMemory to store and retrieve context automatically.
- No manual state tracking is needed, making it scalable for more complex systems.

3. Advanced State Management with Multi-Step Tasks

Let's design an agent that handles a multi-step workflow: processing a customer refund.

Scenario:

1. The agent asks for the order number.
2. Confirms the reason for the refund.
3. Completes the refund process.

Code Example:

```
def refund_agent(user_input, state={"step": 1}):

    if state["step"] == 1:

        state["step"] += 1

        return "Please provide your order
number."


    elif state["step"] == 2:
```

```python
        state["order_number"] = user_input

        state["step"] += 1

        return f"Why do you want to refund order
{state['order_number']}?"


    elif state["step"] == 3:

        state["reason"] = user_input

        state["step"] = 4  # Mark as completed

        return f"Your refund for order
{state['order_number']} is being processed due
to: {state['reason']}."


    return "Your refund has already been
processed."


# Testing the refund process

print(refund_agent("I want a refund."))

print(refund_agent("12345"))

print(refund_agent("Received a defective item."))
```

Expected Output:

Please provide your order number.

Why do you want to refund order 12345?

Your refund for order 12345 is being processed due to: Received a defective item.

Explanation:

- The agent moves through multiple steps, tracking progress with the state dictionary.
- Each input dynamically updates the state, enabling a seamless multi-step process.

Best Practices for Context and State Management

1. Store Only Relevant Data: Avoid tracking unnecessary information to keep the state lightweight and efficient.
2. Use Memory Modules for Scalability: Libraries like LangChain provide scalable memory solutions.
3. Implement Session Management: Separate user sessions to prevent data leakage across users.
4. Ensure Data Privacy: Handle sensitive data carefully and comply with privacy regulations.
5. Handle State Expiry: Clear outdated or irrelevant state data to avoid confusion.

Exercise: Build a Personalized Shopping Assistant

Task:

1. Ask the user for their favorite product category.
2. Remember the preference and suggest products based on it.
3. Handle cases where the user hasn't provided their preference yet.

Hint: Use a state dictionary or LangChain memory to track user preferences.

4.5 Error Handling and Workflow Recovery

In this section, we will explore how to design effective error handling and recovery strategies for AI agents. You will learn how to identify potential failures, handle them gracefully, and design workflows that recover smoothly without frustrating users. I will provide detailed, practical code examples and real-world scenarios to demonstrate these concepts clearly.

Why Error Handling and Workflow Recovery Matter

- Improved User Experience: Graceful error handling prevents users from getting stuck or frustrated.
- System Reliability: Detecting and recovering from failures ensures consistent performance.
- Data Integrity: Protects workflows from incomplete or corrupted data due to failures.
- Scalability: Well-handled errors make it easier to scale systems without breaking

Types of Errors in AI Workflows

1. Input Errors: Invalid or unexpected user inputs (e.g., missing data, wrong formats).
2. API/Service Failures: External services are down or respond with errors.
3. Timeouts: Processes take too long to respond, causing delays or deadlocks.
4. Resource Limits: Memory or computational limits are exceeded.
5. Logical Errors: Bugs or misconfigurations in the workflow logic.

Principles of Effective Error Handling

1. Fail Gracefully: Provide informative and helpful error messages.
2. Retry Strategically: Attempt recovery with controlled retries.
3. Fallback Options: Offer alternatives when preferred solutions fail.
4. Log Errors: Keep detailed logs for diagnosis and monitoring.
5. Isolate Failures: Prevent a small error from cascading and breaking the entire system.

Basic Error Handling in Python

Let's start with a simple example of error handling using Python's try-except block.

Code Example: Handling Division by Zero

```python
def divide_numbers(a, b):

    try:

        result = a / b

        return f"The result is {result}."

    except ZeroDivisionError:

        return "Error: Division by zero is not
allowed."

    except Exception as e:

        return f"An unexpected error occurred:
{e}"



# Testing the function
```

```
print(divide_numbers(10, 2))    # Output: The
result is 5.0.

print(divide_numbers(10, 0))    # Output: Error:
Division by zero is not allowed.
```

Explanation:

- Graceful Error Handling: The program doesn't crash on division by zero.
- General Error Catching: Other unexpected errors are caught and reported.

Error Handling in AI Workflows

In more complex systems, errors can occur at various stages—input processing, external API calls, or model predictions. Let's design an AI agent that handles errors gracefully during a multi-step workflow.

Scenario:

An AI agent assists users with product returns. It needs to:

1. Ask for the order number.
2. Verify the order in the system (simulated by an API call).
3. Process the return request.

Step 1: Simulating External API Failures

```
import random


def verify_order_api(order_number):

    # Simulate API success or failure

    if random.choice([True, False]):
```

```
        return {"status": "success",
"order_number": order_number}

    else:

        raise ConnectionError("Failed to connect
to the order database.")
```

Explanation:

- Sometimes the API call will fail, simulating a real-world scenario where external services are unreliable.

Step 2: Building the Workflow with Error Handling

```
def process_return_workflow(order_number):

    try:

        # Step 1: Verify the order

        order_data =
verify_order_api(order_number)

        print(f"Order
{order_data['order_number']} verified.")



        # Step 2: Process the return

        return "Your return has been successfully
processed."



    except ConnectionError as e:
```

```
        return f"Error: {e}. Please try again
later."


    except Exception as e:

        return f"An unexpected error occurred:
{e}"



# Testing the workflow

print(process_return_workflow("12345"))
```

Expected Output:

If the API succeeds:

 Order 12345 verified.

Your return has been successfully processed.

If the API fails:

 Error: Failed to connect to the order database. Please try again
later.

Explanation:

- The agent informs the user when something goes wrong but does not crash.
- Provides feedback and suggests retrying later.

Implementing Retry Logic

Automatically retrying failed actions can recover from temporary failures. Let's add retries to the order verification step.

Code Example: Retry on Failure

```python
import time


def verify_order_with_retry(order_number,
retries=3):

    for attempt in range(retries):

        try:

            order_data =
verify_order_api(order_number)

            return order_data

        except ConnectionError as e:

            print(f"Attempt {attempt + 1} failed:
{e}")

            if attempt < retries - 1:

                time.sleep(2)  # Wait before
retrying

            else:

                raise ConnectionError("All
attempts to verify the order failed.")


def process_return_workflow(order_number):

    try:

        # Retry order verification
```

```
        order_data =
verify_order_with_retry(order_number)

        print(f"Order
{order_data['order_number']} verified.")

        return "Your return has been successfully
processed."



    except ConnectionError as e:

        return f"Error: {e}. Please try again
later."



print(process_return_workflow("12345"))
```

Explanation:

- If the API fails, the system retries up to 3 times before giving up.
- This improves resilience against temporary network or service disruptions.

Fallback Strategies

If a task repeatedly fails, offering alternative solutions improves user experience.

Code Example: Fallback to Manual Support

```
def process_return_with_fallback(order_number):

    try:
```

```
        order_data =
verify_order_with_retry(order_number)

        print(f"Order
{order_data['order_number']} verified.")

        return "Your return has been successfully
processed."



    except ConnectionError:

        return "We're unable to process your
return right now. Please contact customer support
at support@example.com."



print(process_return_with_fallback("12345"))
```

Explanation:

- When retries fail, the system offers a manual support option instead of leaving the user without help.

Logging Errors for Monitoring

Logging is crucial for diagnosing and fixing recurring issues.

Code Example: Logging Errors

```
def log_error(error_message):

    with open("error_log.txt", "a") as log_file:

        log_file.write(f"{error_message}\n")
```

```python
def process_return_with_logging(order_number):

    try:

        order_data =
verify_order_with_retry(order_number)

        print(f"Order
{order_data['order_number']} verified.")

        return "Your return has been successfully
processed."


    except ConnectionError as e:

        log_error(str(e))

        return "We're experiencing issues. Please
try again later."


print(process_return_with_logging("12345"))
```

Explanation:

- All errors are logged to a file for future analysis.
- Helps developers identify patterns in failures and improve the system.

Best Practices for Error Handling and Recovery

1. Fail Gracefully: Inform users about the problem and suggest actions.
2. Use Retries Wisely: Retry temporary failures but avoid infinite loops.

3. Fallback to Alternatives: Provide backup solutions when primary actions fail.
4. Log Everything: Maintain detailed logs for diagnosing issues.
5. Isolate Failures: Design workflows to contain errors without breaking the entire process.

Exercise: Build a Fault-Tolerant Payment Agent

Task:

1. Simulate a payment processing system with random failures.
2. Add retry logic for temporary failures.
3. If all retries fail, provide a fallback to manual payment assistance.

Chapter 5: Building Real-World Applications

Now that we've covered the foundations of designing intelligent AI agents, it's time to apply these concepts to real-world applications. This chapter focuses on how to build and deploy AI solutions that solve practical problems in various industries.

5.1 Conversational AI and Chatbots

Conversational AI refers to systems that can simulate natural human conversations. This involves understanding user inputs, processing language, and generating appropriate responses. Unlike simple rule-based systems, conversational AI leverages natural language processing (NLP) and machine learning to make interactions more dynamic and adaptive.

Key Components of Conversational AI:

1. Natural Language Understanding (NLU): Interprets the user's input to understand intent and extract relevant information.

2. Dialogue Management: Manages the conversation flow, determining what the system should say or do next.

3. Natural Language Generation (NLG): Produces human-like responses based on the conversation's context and logic.

4. Integration with External Systems: Connects with databases, APIs, or tools to fetch or process data as part of the conversation.

Real-World Applications of Conversational AI

- Customer Support: Automates handling common queries, complaints, and requests.
- E-commerce: Assists customers with product searches, recommendations, and order tracking.
- Healthcare: Schedules appointments, provides medical information, and reminds patients of medications.
- Finance: Handles balance inquiries, transaction histories, and bill payments.
- Productivity Assistants: Manages calendars, sends reminders, and performs task automation.

Types of Chatbots

1. **Rule-Based Chatbots:** Follow predefined scripts and respond to specific commands.
   Example: Pressing "1" for account balance in IVR systems.

2. AI-Powered Chatbots: Use NLP and machine learning to understand and process complex, unstructured inputs.
   Example: Chatbots that understand varied customer service queries.

3. Hybrid Chatbots: Combine rule-based responses with AI to offer flexibility and control.
   Example: A bot that answers FAQs but escalates complex queries to a human agent.

Building a Simple AI-Powered Chatbot

Let's build a basic conversational AI chatbot using LangChain and OpenAI's GPT model.

Step 1: Install Required Libraries

Make sure you have the necessary packages installed:

```
pip install openai langchain python-dotenv
```

Step 2: Configure API Access

Create a .env file in your project folder to store your OpenAI API key securely.

```
OPENAI_API_KEY=your_openai_api_key
```

In your Python script, load the API key:

```
from dotenv import load_dotenv

import os


load_dotenv()

openai_api_key = os.getenv("OPENAI_API_KEY")
```

Step 3: Define the Chatbot

```
from langchain import OpenAI, LLMChain

from langchain.prompts import import PromptTemplate


# Initialize the language model

llm = OpenAI(temperature=0.7)


# Define a prompt template for conversation

chat_prompt = PromptTemplate(
```

```python
    input_variables=["user_message"],

    template="You are a helpful customer support
assistant. Respond to: {user_message}"

)
```

```python
# Create a chain connecting the prompt to the
model

chat_chain = LLMChain(llm=llm,
prompt=chat_prompt)
```

```python
# Chatbot function

def chatbot(user_input):

    return chat_chain.run(user_input)
```

```python
# Testing the chatbot

print(chatbot("Hi, I need help with my order."))

print(chatbot("Can you tell me your return
policy?"))
```

Expected Output:

Sure! I'd be happy to help with your order. Can you please provide your order number?

Our return policy allows returns within 30 days of purchase. Please let me know if you'd like more details.

Explanation:

- The chatbot uses OpenAI's model to generate context-aware, helpful responses.
- The prompt template guides the model to act as a customer support assistant.

Enhancing the Chatbot with Memory

Let's improve the chatbot by enabling it to remember previous interactions. This makes conversations feel more natural and personalized.

Step 1: Add Memory for Context Tracking

```python
from langchain.memory import
ConversationBufferMemory

from langchain.chains import ConversationChain


# Initialize memory to track conversation history

memory = ConversationBufferMemory()


# Create a conversational AI with memory

conversation_chain = ConversationChain(

    llm=llm,

    memory=memory
```

```
)
```

```
# Chatbot with memory

def memory_chatbot(user_input):

    return conversation_chain.run(user_input)
```

```
# Testing the chatbot with memory

print(memory_chatbot("My name is Sarah."))

print(memory_chatbot("What's my name?"))
```

Expected Output:

Nice to meet you, Sarah!

Your name is Sarah.

Explanation:

- The chatbot now remembers user information across interactions.
- ConversationBufferMemory stores past messages, creating a more personalized experience.

Error Handling in Chatbots

It's important to handle unexpected inputs gracefully. Let's improve the chatbot by adding basic error handling.

Code Example: Handling Empty or Invalid Input

```
def robust_chatbot(user_input):
```

```
    if not user_input.strip():

        return "I'm sorry, I didn't catch that.
Could you please rephrase?"

    try:

        response = chat_chain.run(user_input)

        return response

    except Exception as e:

        return f"Oops! Something went wrong: {e}"


# Testing error handling

print(robust_chatbot(""))

print(robust_chatbot("Tell me a joke."))
```

Expected Output:

I'm sorry, I didn't catch that. Could you please rephrase?

Why did the scarecrow win an award? Because he was outstanding in his field!

Explanation:

- The chatbot now gracefully handles empty input or unexpected errors.
- This ensures a better user experience even when something goes wrong.

Integrating the Chatbot with External APIs

To make the chatbot more useful, let's integrate it with an external API for real-time data.

Example: Weather Information Chatbot

```
import requests


def get_weather(city):

    api_key = "your_openweathermap_api_key"

    url =
f"http://api.openweathermap.org/data/2.5/weather?
q={city}&appid={api_key}&units=metric"

    response = requests.get(url)


    if response.status_code == 200:

        data = response.json()

        weather =
data["weather"][0]["description"]

        temperature = data["main"]["temp"]

        return f"The weather in {city} is
{weather} with a temperature of {temperature}°C."

    else:

        return "Sorry, I couldn't retrieve the
weather information right now."
```

```
# Test the weather function

print(get_weather("New York"))
```

Expected Output:

The weather in New York has a clear sky with a temperature of 22°C.

Explanation:

- The chatbot can now provide live weather updates by connecting to the OpenWeather API.
- This makes the chatbot more interactive and informative.

Best Practices for Building Conversational AI

1. Understand User Intent: Use NLU models to extract intent and entities.
2. Keep Conversations Natural: Design responses that sound human-like.
3. Handle Errors Gracefully: Anticipate and manage unexpected inputs.
4. Maintain Context: Use memory to make interactions feel continuous.
5. Secure Sensitive Data: Encrypt and manage user data responsibly.

Exercise: Create a Shopping Assistant Bot

Task:

1. Build a chatbot that helps users find products.
2. Suggest items based on user preferences (e.g., category, price range).
3. Handle invalid input gracefully.

5.2 Knowledge Retrieval and Search Systems

A knowledge retrieval system is designed to search, retrieve, and present relevant information from large datasets, databases, or document collections. These systems use algorithms to match user queries with stored information and return the most relevant results.

Key Components:

1. Data Sources: Documents, databases, articles, or structured data.
2. Indexing: Organizing and optimizing data for quick search and retrieval.
3. Search Algorithms: Methods for matching queries to data (keyword-based or semantic).
4. Ranking Mechanisms: Sorting results by relevance.
5. User Interface (UI): How users interact with the system.

Real-World Applications

- Customer Support: Bots retrieve solutions from FAQs and support manuals.
- Legal Research: Lawyers search case law databases for precedents.
- E-commerce: Product search engines help customers find products.
- Healthcare: Doctors access medical research and patient records.
- Academic Research: Researchers search through scholarly articles.

Types of Search Systems

1. Keyword-Based Search: Matches exact words in the query with stored data.
2. Semantic Search: Understands the intent behind the query and retrieves relevant content.
3. Vector Search (Embedding-Based): Uses machine learning to match the meaning of text.
4. Hybrid Search: Combines keyword and semantic search for higher accuracy.

Building a Basic Keyword Search System

Let's start by creating a simple search system that matches exact words in a document.

Step 1: Load Data

```
documents = [

    "Artificial Intelligence is transforming the
world.",

    "Machine Learning is a subset of Artificial
Intelligence.",

    "Data Science involves data analysis and
visualization.",

    "Deep Learning is a branch of Machine
Learning."

]
```

Step 2: Implement Keyword Search

```
def keyword_search(query, docs):

    results = []
```

```
    for doc in docs:

        if query.lower() in doc.lower():

            results.append(doc)

    return results if results else ["No matching
results found."]



# Testing the search

print(keyword_search("machine learning",
documents))
```

Expected Output:

['Machine Learning is a subset of Artificial Intelligence.',

 'Deep Learning is a branch of Machine Learning.']

Explanation:

- This search system checks if the query string exists in the documents.
- It is simple but struggles with variations in phrasing.

Building a Semantic Search System

Semantic search improves search accuracy by understanding the meaning behind queries rather than relying on exact keywords.

Step 1: Install Required Libraries

pip install openai langchain faiss-cpu

Step 2: Create a Semantic Search System

```python
from langchain.embeddings import OpenAIEmbeddings

from langchain.vectorstores import FAISS


# Initialize the embedding model

embedding_model = OpenAIEmbeddings()


# Create document embeddings

document_embeddings =
embedding_model.embed_documents(documents)


# Build a FAISS search index

search_index = FAISS.from_documents(documents,
embedding_model)


# Semantic search function

def semantic_search(query):

    results =
search_index.similarity_search(query)

    return [result.page_content for result in
results]


# Testing the semantic search
```

```
print(semantic_search("AI in business"))
```

Expected Output:

['Artificial Intelligence is transforming the world.',

'Machine Learning is a subset of Artificial Intelligence.']

Explanation:

- The system retrieves relevant documents even though the query ("AI in business") does not exactly match the content.
- FAISS accelerates similarity searches by comparing vector embeddings.

Comparing Keyword and Semantic Search

Feature	Keyword Search	Semantic Search
Matching Technique	Exact keyword match	Contextual understanding (meaning)
Handling Synonyms	Poor	Strong
Performance	Fast for small datasets	Efficient with vector indexing (FAISS)
Use Cases	Small, structured datasets	Large, unstructured datasets

Scalability	Limited scalability	Scales well with large datasets

Integrating External Knowledge Bases

In real-world scenarios, knowledge isn't always stored in flat files. AI agents need to search through databases, APIs, or external knowledge systems.

Example: Wikipedia Search with LangChain

Let's build a simple tool that retrieves information from Wikipedia.

Step 1: Install Required Package

```
pip install wikipedia
```

Step 2: Create a Wikipedia Search Tool

```
import wikipedia


def wikipedia_search(query):

    try:

        summary = wikipedia.summary(query,
sentences=2)

        return summary

    except
wikipedia.exceptions.DisambiguationError as e:
```

```
      return f"Multiple results found:
{e.options}"

   except wikipedia.exceptions.PageError:

      return "No page found for your query."
```

```
# Testing Wikipedia search

print(wikipedia_search("Artificial
Intelligence"))
```

Expected Output:

Artificial intelligence (AI) is intelligence demonstrated by machines, unlike the natural intelligence displayed by humans and animals. Leading AI textbooks define the field as the study of "intelligent agents."

Explanation:

- The agent can retrieve knowledge from external sources like Wikipedia.
- It handles ambiguous and invalid queries gracefully.

Building a Hybrid Search System

To maximize accuracy, we can combine keyword search and semantic search.

Hybrid Search Code Example

```
def hybrid_search(query, docs):

   # Step 1: Try keyword search

   keyword_results = keyword_search(query, docs)
```

```
    # Step 2: If no keyword matches, use semantic
search

    if keyword_results == ["No matching results
found."]:

        return semantic_search(query)

    return keyword_results


# Testing hybrid search

print(hybrid_search("AI", documents))

print(hybrid_search("neural networks",
documents))
```

Expected Output:

['Artificial Intelligence is transforming the world.',

 'Machine Learning is a subset of Artificial Intelligence.']

['Deep Learning is a branch of Machine Learning.']

Explanation:

- The system first attempts a fast keyword search.
- If no results are found, it uses semantic search for broader matching.

Best Practices for Knowledge Retrieval Systems

1. Choose the Right Search Method: Use keyword search for structured data and semantic search for unstructured content.
2. Optimize for Speed: Use vector databases like FAISS for large datasets.
3. Handle Errors Gracefully: Inform users when data isn't available or when input is invalid.
4. Update Knowledge Regularly: Keep your data sources fresh and accurate.
5. Provide Feedback: Let users know why certain results were returned or not.

Exercise: Build a Domain-Specific Search System

Task:

1. Load a custom dataset (e.g., company policies, product manuals).
2. Implement a hybrid search combining keyword and semantic search.
3. Handle ambiguous or missing queries with clear feedback.

5.3 Business Process Automation

Business Process Automation (BPA) involves using software and technology to automate recurring tasks and workflows in an organization. BPA replaces manual, time-consuming operations with efficient, scalable, and error-free automated processes.

Key Characteristics of BPA:

1. Rule-Based Execution: Automates tasks based on predefined rules and conditions.
2. Scalability: Easily scales with business growth without increasing manual effort.

3. Integration: Connects various tools, systems, and data sources.
4. Consistency: Standardized processes, reducing human errors.

Why Business Process Automation Matters

1. Increased Efficiency: Automating repetitive tasks frees employees to focus on high-value work, speeding up operations.

2. Cost Savings: Reduces labor costs and operational expenses by minimizing manual work.

3. Error Reduction: Automation minimizes human errors, ensuring greater accuracy and consistency.

4. Better Compliance: Ensures that business processes align with regulatory requirements by enforcing standardized workflows.

5. Scalability: Automated processes can handle larger workloads without needing proportional human resources.

Real-World Applications of BPA

- Finance: Automating invoice processing, expense approvals, and payroll management.
- Human Resources (HR): Automating employee onboarding, leave requests, and performance reviews.
- Customer Support: Handling common queries, routing tickets, and updating customer records.
- Sales and Marketing: Automating lead generation, email campaigns, and customer engagement.
- Supply Chain: Managing inventory, order processing, and shipment tracking.

Building a Simple Business Process Automation

Let's create a basic automation system that processes customer orders. This system will:

1. Validate the order.
2. Check inventory.
3. Process payment.
4. Confirm the order.

Step 1: Automating Order Processing

```
# Step 1: Validate Order

def validate_order(order):

    if "product" in order and "quantity" in
order:

        return True

    return False



# Step 2: Check Inventory

def check_inventory(product, quantity):

    stock = {"laptop": 5, "mouse": 10,
"keyboard": 2}

    return stock.get(product, 0) >= quantity



# Step 3: Process Payment

def process_payment(amount):
```

```python
    return "Payment successful!" if amount > 0
else "Payment failed."



# Step 4: Confirm Order

def confirm_order(order):

    return f"Order confirmed for
{order['quantity']} {order['product']}(s)."



# Complete Automation Workflow

def automate_order(order):

    if not validate_order(order):

        return "Invalid order. Please check the
details."


    if not check_inventory(order["product"],
order["quantity"]):

        return "Insufficient stock. Please reduce
the quantity."


    payment_status =
process_payment(order["quantity"] * 1000)   #
Assume unit price is $1000

    if payment_status != "Payment successful!":
```

```
        return payment_status



    return confirm_order(order)



# Testing the workflow

order_1 = {"product": "laptop", "quantity": 2}

order_2 = {"product": "keyboard", "quantity": 5}



print(automate_order(order_1))

print(automate_order(order_2))
```

Expected Output:

Order confirmed for 2 laptop(s).

Insufficient stock. Please reduce the quantity.

Explanation:

- The system checks if the order is valid, verifies stock, processes payment, and confirms the order.
- This is a streamlined example of how a typical e-commerce workflow can be automated.

Advanced BPA with Task Automation and Scheduling

Let's automate a daily task: generating and emailing a sales report.

Step 1: Install Required Packages

```
pip install pandas openpyxl schedule
```

Step 2: Generate and Email a Sales Report

```python
import pandas as pd

import smtplib

import schedule

import time


# Step 1: Generate Sales Report

def generate_sales_report():

    sales_data = {

        'Product': ['Laptop', 'Mouse',
'Keyboard'],

        'Units Sold': [50, 120, 35],

        'Revenue': [50000, 2400, 3500]

    }


    df = pd.DataFrame(sales_data)

    df.to_excel("daily_sales_report.xlsx",
index=False)

    print("Sales report generated.")


# Step 2: Send Report via Email
```

```python
def send_email():

    sender = "your_email@example.com"

    receiver = "manager@example.com"

    password = "your_password"


    subject = "Daily Sales Report"

    body = "Please find attached the daily sales
report."


    # Connect to the server

    server = smtplib.SMTP("smtp.example.com",
587)

    server.starttls()

    server.login(sender, password)


    message = f"Subject: {subject}\n\n{body}"

    server.sendmail(sender, receiver, message)

    server.quit()

    print("Email sent successfully.")


# Step 3: Automate with Scheduling
```

```python
def daily_task():

    generate_sales_report()

    send_email()


# Schedule the task every day at 6 PM

schedule.every().day.at("18:00").do(daily_task)


# Keep the script running

while True:

    schedule.run_pending()

    time.sleep(60)
```

Explanation:

- Sales Report Generation: Automatically generates a report as an Excel file.
- Email Notification: Sends the report via email.
- Task Scheduling: Runs this task daily at 6 PM without manual intervention.

Automating Approval Workflows

Many businesses require approvals for tasks like budget approvals, time-off requests, or purchase orders. Let's automate a leave approval workflow.

Code Example: Leave Approval Automation

```python
def leave_request(employee, days_requested):
```

```
max_leave_days = 20

if days_requested <= max_leave_days:

    return f"Leave approved for {employee}."

else:

    return f"Leave request denied for {employee}. Please
contact HR."



# Testing the approval process

print(leave_request("Alice", 15))

print(leave_request("Bob", 25))
```

Expected Output:

Leave approved for Alice.

Leave request denied for Bob. Please contact HR.

Explanation:

- The system automates the decision-making for leave approvals based on company policy.
- This can be expanded with email notifications and multi-level approvals.

Best Practices for Business Process Automation

1. Start Small: Automate simple, repetitive tasks before moving on to complex workflows.
2. Identify Bottlenecks: Focus on areas that slow down business operations.

3. Integrate Systems: Ensure different tools and software can communicate.
4. Maintain Flexibility: Design workflows that can adapt to business changes.
5. Monitor and Improve: Continuously monitor automated workflows and optimize them.

Exercise: Automate Invoice Processing

Task:

1. Read invoice data from a CSV file.
2. Validate the invoice details.
3. Automatically send payment confirmation emails.
4. Log any errors for failed invoices.

Business Process Automation simplifies and streamlines operations by eliminating repetitive tasks, reducing errors, and enhancing productivity. Whether it's automating order processing, report generation, or approval workflows, BPA is an essential tool for modern organizations.

5.4 Data Analysis and Reporting Agents

In the data-driven world we live in, businesses rely heavily on data analysis to make informed decisions, predict trends, and monitor performance. However, manually analyzing data and creating reports can be time-consuming and error-prone. This is where Data Analysis and Reporting Agents come in. These agents automate data processing, analysis, and reporting, enabling organizations to extract insights efficiently and accurately.

Data Analysis and Reporting Agents are automated systems designed to:

1. Collect Data from various sources.

2. Process and Analyze the data to identify patterns, trends, and insights.
3. Generate Reports that summarize findings in a clear, actionable format.
4. Distribute Reports via emails, dashboards, or cloud storage.

These agents can operate on schedules or in real-time, providing continuous insights without human intervention.

Why Use Data Analysis and Reporting Agents?

1. Efficiency: They automate repetitive tasks like data cleaning, analysis, and reporting, saving significant time.

2. Accuracy: By eliminating manual steps, they reduce the chances of human error in data processing.

3. Real-Time Insights: They can provide instant analysis and reporting, enabling faster decision-making.

4. Scalability: Agents can handle large datasets and complex analyses more efficiently than manual processes.

5. Cost Reduction: Automating reporting tasks reduces labor costs and allows teams to focus on higher-value work.

Real-World Applications

- Sales Reporting: Automating daily, weekly, and monthly sales performance reports.
- Financial Analysis: Generating profit/loss statements, forecasting, and expense tracking.
- Marketing Analytics: Analyzing campaign performance and customer engagement.
- Operations Monitoring: Tracking supply chain metrics and production data.

- Healthcare Reporting: Monitoring patient data and generating compliance reports.

Building a Data Analysis and Reporting Agent

Let's build a data analysis agent that reads sales data, analyzes performance, and generates a report. We will use Python and Pandas for data analysis and automate report generation with Matplotlib and email delivery.

Step 1: Install Required Libraries

```
pip install pandas matplotlib openpyxl
```

Step 2: Sample Sales Data

Let's assume we have a CSV file, sales_data.csv, with the following structure:

Date	Product	Units Sold	Revenue
2024-01-01	Laptop	5	5000
2024-01-01	Keyboard	10	1000
2024-01-02	Laptop	3	3000
2024-01-02	Mouse	15	750

Step 3: Analyzing Sales Data

```python
import pandas as pd


# Load the sales data
def load_sales_data(file_path):

    return pd.read_csv(file_path)


# Analyze total sales and revenue
def analyze_sales(df):

    total_units = df['Units Sold'].sum()

    total_revenue = df['Revenue'].sum()

    top_product =
df.groupby('Product')['Revenue'].sum().idxmax()


    analysis = {

        "Total Units Sold": total_units,

        "Total Revenue": total_revenue,

        "Top Selling Product": top_product

    }

    return analysis
```

```
# Testing the analysis

sales_df = load_sales_data("sales_data.csv")

analysis_results = analyze_sales(sales_df)

print(analysis_results)
```

Expected Output:

{'Total Units Sold': 33, 'Total Revenue': 9750, 'Top Selling Product': 'Laptop'}

Explanation:

- The agent loads sales data, calculates the total units sold, total revenue, and identifies the top-selling product.

Step 4: Generating a Visual Sales Report

Let's create a bar chart of product-wise revenue.

```
import matplotlib.pyplot as plt


def generate_sales_report(df):

                                product_sales      =
df.groupby('Product')['Revenue'].sum()


    # Create a bar chart

                    product_sales.plot(kind='bar',
color='skyblue')

    plt.xlabel('Product')
```

```python
    plt.ylabel('Revenue')

    plt.title('Revenue by Product')

    plt.tight_layout()

    plt.savefig('sales_report.png')

    plt.close()

        print("Sales    report    generated    as
'sales_report.png'.")



# Generate the report

generate_sales_report(sales_df)
```

Explanation:

- This function generates a bar chart showing revenue for each product and saves it as an image.
- Visualizations make reports more insightful and easier to interpret.

Step 5: Automating Report Delivery via Email

Let's send the generated report as an email attachment.

```python
import smtplib

from email.message import EmailMessage


def send_email_report():

    sender = "your_email@example.com"
```

```python
receiver = "manager@example.com"

password = "your_password"


# Create the email

msg = EmailMessage()

msg['Subject'] = 'Daily Sales Report'

msg['From'] = sender

msg['To'] = receiver

msg.set_content("Please find the attached
sales report.")


# Attach the report image

with open("sales_report.png", "rb") as file:

    msg.add_attachment(file.read(),
maintype='image', subtype='png',
filename="sales_report.png")


# Connect to the server and send the email

with smtplib.SMTP('smtp.example.com', 587) as
server:

    server.starttls()

    server.login(sender, password)
```

```
    server.send_message(msg)

    print("Sales report sent via email.")


# Send the report

send_email_report()
```

Explanation:

- The report is automatically emailed to stakeholders.
- This eliminates the need for manual report sharing.

Advanced Data Analysis: Forecasting Sales

Let's add a forecasting feature using **linear regression** to predict future sales.

```
from sklearn.linear_model import LinearRegression

import numpy as np


def forecast_sales(df):

    # Prepare data

    df['Date'] = pd.to_datetime(df['Date'])

    df['Day'] = df['Date'].dt.day

    X = df[['Day']]

    y = df['Revenue']
```

```
# Train the model

model = LinearRegression()

model.fit(X, y)


# Predict future sales

future_days = np.array([[3], [4], [5]])

predictions = model.predict(future_days)


    forecast = dict(zip(future_days.flatten(),
predictions.round(2)))

    return forecast


# Forecast sales

forecast_results = forecast_sales(sales_df)

print("Sales Forecast:", forecast_results)
```

Expected Output:

Sales Forecast: {3: 3500.0, 4: 4000.0, 5: 4500.0}

Explanation:

- The agent uses linear regression to forecast future revenue based on historical data.
- This feature helps businesses plan better by predicting future trends.

Best Practices for Data Analysis and Reporting Agents

1. Automate the Entire Pipeline: From data collection to analysis and report delivery.
2. Use Visuals Wisely: Incorporate charts and graphs for clearer insights.
3. Ensure Data Accuracy: Validate data before processing.
4. Schedule Reports: Use schedulers to run reports daily, weekly, or monthly.
5. Secure Sensitive Data: Encrypt reports and secure communication channels.

Exercise: Build a Weekly Performance Report Agent

Task:

1. Load weekly performance data from a CSV file.
2. Analyze KPIs like revenue growth, customer engagement, and conversion rates.
3. Generate visual reports and automate email delivery every Monday.

5.5 Custom Tool Integration for Specialized Tasks

Custom tool integration involves connecting external software tools, APIs, and systems to AI agents to perform specialized tasks. This extends the agent's capabilities beyond basic processing by leveraging external data, services, or hardware.

Key Components of Custom Integration:

1. External Tools/APIs: Services like payment gateways, CRMs, or IoT devices.
2. AI Agent Logic: The decision-making system that orchestrates tools.

3. Data Flow: How data moves between the agent and integrated tools.
4. Error Handling: Managing failures in external tools gracefully.
5. Security: Protecting sensitive data during integration.

Why Custom Tool Integration Matters

1. Tailored Workflows: Generic solutions often don't cover niche requirements. Custom integrations enable building workflows specific to business needs.

2. Automation of Specialized Tasks: Repetitive and complex tasks like document processing, data synchronization, and real-time monitoring can be fully automated.

3. Enhanced Functionality: Custom tools allow AI agents to access advanced capabilities, such as interacting with IoT devices or financial services.

4. Competitive Advantage: Unique integrations can streamline operations, improve customer experience, and differentiate your business.

Real-World Examples of Custom Tool Integration

- E-commerce: Integrating payment gateways, inventory systems, and shipping services.
- Healthcare: Connecting to electronic health records (EHRs) and medical devices.
- Finance: Automating compliance checks with regulatory databases.
- Manufacturing: Monitoring and controlling production lines via IoT sensors.

- Marketing: Synchronizing customer data with CRM platforms for personalized marketing.

Building a Custom Tool Integration

Let's build a custom integration where an AI agent processes customer orders and interacts with external services for payment and shipping.

Scenario:

1. Process a customer order.
2. Charge the customer using a mock payment API.
3. Arrange shipping through a mock logistics API.

Step 1: Mock Payment API Integration

```python
import random



# Mock payment processing function

def process_payment(order_id, amount):

    # Simulate payment success or failure

    if random.choice([True, False]):

        return {"status": "success",
"transaction_id":
f"TXN{random.randint(1000,9999)}"}

    else:

        return {"status": "failed", "reason":
"Insufficient funds"}
```

```python
# Test payment processing

payment_result =
process_payment(order_id="ORD1234",
amount=150.00)

print(payment_result)
```

Expected Output:

```
{'status': 'success', 'transaction_id':
'TXN1234'}
```

or

```
{'status': 'failed', 'reason': 'Insufficient
funds'}
```

Explanation:

- The agent simulates calling a payment gateway API.
- It handles success and failure responses to maintain workflow continuity.

Step 2: Mock Shipping API Integration

```python
def arrange_shipping(order_id, address):

    # Simulate shipping arrangement

    tracking_id =
f"SHIP{random.randint(10000,99999)}"

    return {"status": "shipped", "tracking_id":
tracking_id, "address": address}
```

```
# Test shipping arrangement

shipping_result =
arrange_shipping(order_id="ORD1234", address="123
Main St, NY")

print(shipping_result)
```

Expected Output:

{'status': 'shipped', 'tracking_id': 'SHIP45678', 'address': '123 Main St, NY'}

Explanation:

- This simulates an integration with a shipping/logistics API.
- It returns tracking information for the order.

Step 3: Automating the Workflow

Now, let's combine payment and shipping into a seamless workflow.

```
def order_fulfillment(order_id, amount, address):

    # Step 1: Process payment

    payment = process_payment(order_id, amount)


    if payment['status'] == 'failed':

        return f"Order {order_id} failed:
{payment['reason']}"
```

```python
    # Step 2: Arrange shipping

    shipping = arrange_shipping(order_id,
address)


    # Step 3: Confirm order

    return (f"Order {order_id} confirmed!\n"

        f"Transaction ID:
{payment['transaction_id']}\n"

        f"Shipping Tracking ID:
{shipping['tracking_id']}")


# Testing the full workflow

print(order_fulfillment("ORD1234", 150.00, "123
Main St, NY"))
```

Expected Output:

Order ORD1234 confirmed!

Transaction ID: TXN5678

Shipping Tracking ID: SHIP98765

or if payment fails:

Order ORD1234 failed: Insufficient funds

Explanation:

- The agent integrates both **payment** and **shipping services**.
- Errors (e.g., payment failures) are handled gracefully, preventing workflow breakdown.

Advanced Custom Integration: External API with Authentication

Many real-world APIs require authentication. Let's simulate integrating a **currency exchange API** with authentication.

Step 1: Install Requests Library

```
pip install requests
```

Step 2: Currency Conversion API Integration

```python
import requests


def convert_currency(amount, from_currency,
to_currency, api_key):

    url =
f"https://api.exchangerate-api.com/v4/latest/{fro
m_currency}"

    headers = {"Authorization": f"Bearer
{api_key}"}


    response = requests.get(url, headers=headers)
```

```python
    if response.status_code == 200:

        rate =
response.json()["rates"][to_currency]

        converted_amount = amount * rate

        return f"{amount} {from_currency} =
{converted_amount:.2f} {to_currency}"

    else:

        return "Error: Unable to fetch currency
rates."



# Testing currency conversion

api_key = "your_api_key_here"

print(convert_currency(100, "USD", "EUR",
api_key))
```

Explanation:

- This function integrates with an authenticated external API to convert currencies.
- In real-world systems, such integrations automate financial operations across currencies.

Best Practices for Custom Tool Integration

1. Understand API Documentation: Study the external tool's API thoroughly before integration.
2. Secure Credentials: Use environment variables or vaults to store sensitive information (e.g., API keys).
3. Implement Error Handling: Always handle failed API calls gracefully.

4. Rate Limiting: Respect API rate limits to avoid being blocked.
5. Monitor Integrations: Log errors and monitor API performance regularly.

Exercise: Automate Inventory Management

Task:

1. Connect to a mock inventory API to check stock levels.
2. Automatically reorder products if the stock falls below a threshold.
3. Send a notification when the order is placed.

Chapter 6: Advanced Techniques in LangChain and LangGraph

As you continue to build more sophisticated AI workflows, it becomes essential to master advanced techniques that enhance the efficiency, adaptability, and security of your systems. LangChain and LangGraph offer powerful tools that go beyond basic automation and agent design, allowing you to develop intelligent systems that are context-aware, scalable, and optimized for performance. In this chapter, we'll explore several advanced strategies for making your LangChain and LangGraph workflows more robust and effective

6.1 Memory and Context Management in Agents

In real-world applications, the effectiveness of AI agents often depends on their ability to remember past interactions and maintain context throughout a conversation or workflow. This is what transforms an AI agent from a simple question-answer bot into an intelligent system that can carry out complex tasks, make decisions based on historical data, and engage users in meaningful interactions.

Why Memory and Context Matter in AI Agents

Without memory, an AI agent treats every interaction as a new conversation. This severely limits its ability to:

1. Hold Coherent Conversations: Users expect an agent to remember details like their name, preferences, or previous questions.

2. Execute Multi-Step Tasks: Complex workflows often require agents to track progress across multiple steps.

3. Provide Personalized Experiences: Remembering user preferences helps tailor responses and recommendations.

4. Adapt Over Time: Long-term memory allows agents to improve by learning from past interactions.

Types of Memory in AI Agents

1. Short-Term Memory (Session Memory)

- Stores information during a single session or interaction.
- Useful for tracking conversation flow or multi-step processes.
- Discarded after the session ends.

Example Use Case:
A customer service chatbot that remembers the user's issue during a chat but resets when the conversation ends.

2. Long-Term Memory (Persistent Memory)

- Retains information across multiple sessions.
- Allows for personalization and learning over time.

Example Use Case:
A shopping assistant that remembers past purchases and recommends products accordingly.

3. Episodic Memory

- Remembers specific past events or interactions in detail.
- Useful for reviewing past tasks or conversations.

Example Use Case:
 A virtual assistant that recalls your previous meeting notes when you ask for a summary.

4. Semantic Memory

- Stores facts and general knowledge.
- Independent of specific past experiences.

Example Use Case:
 An AI tutor that remembers educational concepts and can explain them without relying on past interactions.

Implementing Memory in LangChain

LangChain provides built-in memory components that make it easy to integrate memory into AI workflows. Let's explore how to use these effectively.

Example 1: Short-Term Memory with ConversationBufferMemory

This memory type stores the ongoing conversation during a single session.

Code Example: Basic Chatbot with Short-Term Memory

```
from langchain import OpenAI, ConversationChain

from langchain.memory import
ConversationBufferMemory


# Initialize the language model

llm = OpenAI(temperature=0.7)
```

```
# Set up short-term memory

memory = ConversationBufferMemory()


# Create a conversational chain with memory

conversation = ConversationChain(llm=llm,
memory=memory)


# Simulate a conversation

print(conversation.run("Hello, my name is
John."))

print(conversation.run("What's my name?"))
```

Expected Output:

Hello John! How can I help you today?

Your name is John.

Explanation:

- The chatbot remembers the user's name during the session.
- This memory is temporary and resets when the session ends.

Example 2: Long-Term Memory with
ConversationSummaryMemory

This memory type summarizes past interactions for long-term retention.

Code Example: Persistent Memory

```python
from langchain.memory import
ConversationSummaryMemory


# Initialize long-term memory

long_term_memory =
ConversationSummaryMemory(llm=llm)


# Create a conversational chain with long-term
memory

persistent_conversation =
ConversationChain(llm=llm,
memory=long_term_memory)


# Simulate an extended conversation

print(persistent_conversation.run("Hi, I just
moved to New York."))

print(persistent_conversation.run("Can you
suggest places to visit in my city?"))
```

Expected Output:

Welcome to New York! I'd recommend visiting Central Park, the Metropolitan Museum of Art, and the Statue of Liberty.

Explanation:

- The agent remembers that the user is in New York and tailors recommendations accordingly.
- This memory persists beyond the current session.

Example 3: Custom Memory for Multi-Step Task Tracking

For complex workflows, custom memory can track the progress of multi-step tasks.

Code Example: Multi-Step Order Process

```python
# Define custom memory for order tracking

order_memory = {}


def order_process(user_input):

    if "order" in user_input.lower():

        order_memory['step'] = 'awaiting product'

        return "What product would you like to order?"

    elif order_memory.get('step') == 'awaiting product':

        order_memory['product'] = user_input

        order_memory['step'] = 'awaiting quantity'

        return f"How many {user_input} would you like to order?"

    elif order_memory.get('step') == 'awaiting quantity':

        order_memory['quantity'] = user_input

        order_memory['step'] = 'completed'
```

```
        return f"Order confirmed:
{order_memory['quantity']}
{order_memory['product']}(s)."

    else:

        return "Would you like to place an
order?"


# Simulate the order process

print(order_process("I want to place an order."))

print(order_process("Laptops"))

print(order_process("3"))
```

Expected Output:

What product would you like to order?

How many Laptops would you like to order?

Order confirmed: 3 Laptops.

Explanation:

- The agent tracks the user's progress through the order process.
- It remembers responses across multiple steps until the task is complete.

Challenges in Memory and Context Management

1. Memory Overload: Storing too much context can slow down responses.

Solution: Use summarized memory for long interactions.

2. Privacy Concerns: Sensitive information must be handled carefully.

 Solution: Encrypt data and limit retention.

3. Context Relevance: Not all information should be remembered.
Solution: Implement filters to store only relevant details.

4. Data Consistency: Information stored across sessions must be accurate.

Solution: Validate and update memory regularly.

Best Practices for Memory Management

1. Use Appropriate Memory Types: Match memory design to the use case (short-term vs. long-term).

2. Summarize Conversations: Summarize large conversations to avoid memory overload.

3. Secure Sensitive Data: Encrypt user data and comply with privacy regulations.

4. Contextual Relevance: Store only information that improves user experience.

5. Test for Continuity: Regularly test that the agent maintains and applies context correctly.

Exercise: Enhance a Personal Assistant with Memory

Task:

1. Implement an AI assistant that remembers the user's name, preferences, and tasks.
2. Store task lists and recall them across sessions.
3. Add error handling for forgotten or unclear inputs.

6.2 Dynamic Tool Selection and Adaptation

In the rapidly evolving world of artificial intelligence, flexibility is critical. AI agents need to perform a wide range of tasks, and no single tool can handle everything efficiently. This is where dynamic tool selection and adaptation come into play. It allows AI agents to intelligently select the most appropriate tool for a task, adapt to different situations, and provide accurate, efficient solutions.

Dynamic Tool Selection enables an AI agent to intelligently choose the most suitable tool for a given task or user request.
Adaptation allows the agent to adjust its behavior based on context, data, or changing user needs.

Key Characteristics:

1. Flexibility: Agents can handle a wide variety of tasks by selecting different tools.
2. Efficiency: Reduces processing time by avoiding unnecessary tools or actions.
3. Scalability: New tools can be integrated seamlessly without redesigning the entire system.
4. Adaptability: Agents adjust their strategies based on user input or environmental changes.

Why Dynamic Tool Selection is Essential

1. Task Variety: Users may request tasks ranging from calculations to data retrieval to content generation. A single tool can't handle all these efficiently.

2. Performance Optimization: Not every tool is needed for every query. Dynamically selecting the right one saves resources and speeds up responses.

3. Customization and Personalization: Different users may have different needs. Adaptive tool selection ensures personalized service.

4. Seamless Integration: New tools or services can be integrated into the system without affecting existing workflows.

Real-World Applications

- Virtual Assistants: Choosing between scheduling tools, calculators, or web search depending on the request.
- E-commerce Platforms: Switching between recommendation engines, inventory checkers, or payment gateways.
- Customer Support Chatbots: Selecting between FAQ databases, live support escalation, or troubleshooting guides.
- Financial Tools: Dynamically picking between stock analysis, currency conversion, or risk assessment models.

Building Dynamic Tool Selection with LangChain

LangChain makes it straightforward to implement dynamic tool selection by allowing agents to choose from multiple tools based on user input.

Example Scenario:

An AI assistant can perform three tasks:

1. Basic math calculations.
2. Weather forecasting.

3. Telling jokes.

Step 1: Install Required Packages

pip install openai langchain requests

Step 2: Define the Tools

Let's create three distinct tools for our assistant.

```
from langchain.agents import Tool


# Tool 1: Calculator
def calculator_tool(input_text):
    try:
        result = eval(input_text)
        return f"The result is {result}."
    except Exception:
        return "Sorry, I couldn't calculate
that."


# Tool 2: Weather Info (Mock)
def weather_tool(input_text):
    city = input_text.split("in")[-1].strip()
    return f"The weather in {city} is sunny with
a high of 25°C."   # Mock response
```

```
# Tool 3: Joke Generator

def joke_tool(_):

    return "Why did the computer catch a cold?
Because it forgot to close its Windows!"



# Wrapping the tools

calculator = Tool(name="Calculator",
func=calculator_tool, description="Performs math
calculations.")

weather = Tool(name="Weather", func=weather_tool,
description="Provides weather information.")

joke = Tool(name="Joke", func=joke_tool,
description="Tells a random joke.")
```

Explanation:

- Calculator Tool: Handles basic math.
- Weather Tool: Provides mock weather updates.
- Joke Tool: Responds with a joke.

Step 3: Initialize the Agent with Dynamic Tool Selection

```
from langchain import OpenAI

from langchain.agents import initialize_agent



# Initialize the language model
```

```
llm = OpenAI(temperature=0.7)


# Create an agent with dynamic tool selection

agent = initialize_agent(

    tools=[calculator, weather, joke],

    llm=llm,

    agent_type="zero-shot-react-description"

)


# Testing the agent

print(agent.run("What is 15 * 4?"))

print(agent.run("Tell me a joke."))

print(agent.run("What's the weather in New
York?"))
```

Expected Output:

The result is 60.

Why did the computer catch a cold? Because it forgot to close its Windows!

The weather in New York is sunny with a high of 25°C.

Explanation:

- The agent dynamically selects the right tool based on the query.

- Math query → Calculator Tool
- Joke request → Joke Tool
- Weather query → Weather Tool

Advanced Example: Context-Aware Tool Adaptation

Let's take this further by allowing the agent to **adapt its tool selection** based on context.

Scenario:

If a user has already asked about the weather, the agent should prioritize providing related suggestions (e.g., travel tips) instead of repeating weather information.

Step 1: Add Contextual Memory

```
from langchain.memory import
ConversationBufferMemory


# Initialize memory for context tracking

memory = ConversationBufferMemory()


Step 2: Adapt Tool Behavior Based on Context

def adaptive_weather_tool(input_text):

    if "rain" in input_text.lower():

        return "It might rain today. Don't forget
your umbrella!"

    return weather_tool(input_text)
```

```python
adaptive_weather = Tool(name="Adaptive Weather",
func=adaptive_weather_tool,    description="Gives
weather advice.")


# Initialize agent with adaptive tool

adaptive_agent = initialize_agent(

    tools=[calculator, adaptive_weather, joke],

    llm=llm,

    memory=memory,

    agent_type="zero-shot-react-description"

)


# Testing adaptive behavior

print(adaptive_agent.run("What's the weather in
London?"))

print(adaptive_agent.run("Will it rain today?"))
```

Expected Output:

The weather in London is sunny with a high of 25°C.

It might rain today. Don't forget your umbrella!

Explanation:

- The agent remembers the previous query and adapts its response.
- It doesn't just report weather—it proactively gives contextual advice.

Challenges in Dynamic Tool Selection

1. Ambiguity in User Input: If the input is vague, the agent may choose the wrong tool.
Solution: Use clarifying questions or fallbacks.

2. Too Many Tools: More tools can slow down selection or increase confusion.
Solution: Organize tools into categories and prioritize.

3. Conflicting Tools: Multiple tools might be suitable for the same query.
Solution: Assign priority levels or implement decision logic.

Best Practices for Dynamic Tool Selection

1. Clear Tool Descriptions: Define each tool's purpose clearly for accurate selection.
2. Prioritization: Assign importance to tools for similar tasks.
3. Context Awareness: Use memory to adapt tools based on previous interactions.
4. Error Handling: Gracefully handle tool failures or incorrect selections.
5. Scalable Design: Structure tools modularly for easy updates and additions.

Exercise: Build a Multi-Functional AI Assistant

Task:

1. Create an AI assistant with these tools:

- Unit Converter (e.g., inches to centimeters)
- News Fetcher (mocked news headlines)
- Currency Converter (mock rates)
2. Implement dynamic selection for user queries.
3. Add context-awareness to suggest relevant tools.

6.3 Parallel Processing and Workflow Optimization

As AI systems grow more complex and handle larger datasets or workflows, performance becomes a critical factor. Long response times, bottlenecks, and inefficient resource usage can degrade the user experience and limit the scalability of your solutions. This is where Parallel Processing and Workflow Optimization come into play. These techniques are essential for creating high-performance AI systems that can scale smoothly and respond quickly.

Why Parallel Processing and Workflow Optimization Matter

1. Speed and Efficiency: Sequential workflows often lead to delays, especially when handling large datasets or complex tasks. Parallel processing allows multiple tasks to run simultaneously, drastically reducing execution time.

2. Scalability: Optimized workflows can handle increased loads without requiring proportional increases in computing resources.

3. Resource Utilization: Efficient workflows make better use of CPU, memory, and I/O, leading to cost savings and faster response times.

4. User Experience: Faster responses and smooth performance lead to better user engagement and satisfaction.

Understanding Parallel Processing

Parallel Processing involves breaking tasks into smaller sub-tasks and executing them at the same time across multiple processors or threads.

Types of Parallel Processing:

1. Task Parallelism: Different tasks run simultaneously.
2. Data Parallelism: The same task is applied to different data chunks in parallel.
3. Pipeline Parallelism: Tasks are broken into stages and executed in a pipeline, with multiple stages running concurrently.

Real-World Examples:

- E-commerce: Processing thousands of product images simultaneously for resizing and optimization.
- Chatbots: Handling multiple user queries at once without delay.
- Data Processing: Aggregating data from multiple APIs in real-time.

Parallel Processing with Python

Python provides several ways to implement parallel processing:

- Threading: For I/O-bound tasks.
- Multiprocessing: For CPU-bound tasks.
- Asynchronous Programming (asyncio): For concurrent I/O-bound workflows.

Choosing the Right Approach:

- I/O-bound tasks: Use asyncio or threading (e.g., web scraping, API calls).

- CPU-bound tasks: Use multiprocessing (e.g., data processing, machine learning training).

Implementing Parallel Processing

1. Parallel API Requests with asyncio: Fetching data from multiple APIs is a common bottleneck. Let's parallelize it.

```python
import asyncio

import aiohttp


# Async function to fetch data from a URL

async def fetch(session, url):

    async with session.get(url) as response:

        return await response.text()


# Parallel API calls

async def fetch_multiple(urls):

    async with aiohttp.ClientSession() as session:

        tasks = [fetch(session, url) for url in urls]

        return await asyncio.gather(*tasks)


# URLs to fetch data from
```

```
urls = [

    "https://jsonplaceholder.typicode.com/posts/1",

    "https://jsonplaceholder.typicode.com/posts/2",

    "https://jsonplaceholder.typicode.com/posts/3"

]


# Run the async tasks

results = asyncio.run(fetch_multiple(urls))

for i, result in enumerate(results, 1):

    print(f"Result {i}: {result[:100]}...")   #
Print first 100 characters
```

Expected Output:

(Partial data from the APIs)

Result 1: { "userId": 1, "id": 1, "title": "Sample title 1"...

Result 2: { "userId": 1, "id": 2, "title": "Sample title 2"...

Result 3: { "userId": 1, "id": 3, "title": "Sample title 3"...

Explanation:

- All API requests run simultaneously, reducing the total wait time.
- asyncio.gather executes tasks concurrently.

2. CPU-Bound Processing with multiprocessing

Let's speed up a CPU-intensive task—calculating the squares of large numbers.

```python
from multiprocessing import Pool

import time


# Function to compute the square

def compute_square(n):

    return n * n


# List of numbers

numbers = list(range(1, 10_000_001))


# Sequential processing

start_time = time.time()

result = list(map(compute_square, numbers))

print(f"Sequential Time: {time.time() -
start_time:.2f} seconds")


# Parallel processing

start_time = time.time()
```

```
with Pool() as pool:

    result = pool.map(compute_square, numbers)

print(f"Parallel Time: {time.time() -
start_time:.2f} seconds")
```

Expected Output:

Sequential Time: 4.85 seconds

Parallel Time: 1.23 seconds

Explanation:

- Parallel processing significantly reduces the computation time.
- The Pool automatically distributes tasks across CPU cores.

Workflow Optimization Strategies

1. Task Prioritization: Identify critical tasks and prioritize their execution.

Example: Processing urgent customer orders before general inquiries.

2. Batch Processing: Process data in chunks to reduce overhead.

Example: Instead of processing every incoming data point, process them in batches of 100.

3. Asynchronous Workflows: Offload I/O-bound tasks asynchronously to avoid blocking.

Example: Sending emails asynchronously after order confirmation.

4. Caching: Store frequently used results to avoid redundant processing.

Example: Cache product recommendations for returning users.

LangGraph for Parallel Workflow Execution

LangGraph enables creating complex workflows where tasks can be executed in parallel. Let's automate a data pipeline that involves fetching data, cleaning it, and generating reports.

```python
import asyncio


async def fetch_data():

    await asyncio.sleep(2)

    return "Fetched Data"


async def clean_data():

    await asyncio.sleep(3)

    return "Cleaned Data"


async def generate_report():

    await asyncio.sleep(1)

    return "Generated Report"


async def workflow():
```

```
    tasks = [fetch_data(), clean_data(),
generate_report()]

    results = await asyncio.gather(*tasks)

    return results



# Run the optimized workflow

result = asyncio.run(workflow())

print(result)
```

Expected Output:

['Fetched Data', 'Cleaned Data', 'Generated Report']

Explanation:

- All tasks run **simultaneously**.
- Total workflow time is about **3 seconds**, not 6, because of parallel execution.

Best Practices for Workflow Optimization

1. Profile First: Identify bottlenecks using profiling tools (e.g., cProfile).
2. Balance Parallelism: Too many parallel tasks can overwhelm the system.
3. Avoid Overhead: Keep parallel tasks substantial; small tasks may suffer from context-switching overhead.
4. Use Caching Wisely: Cache only data that's costly to compute or fetch.
5. Graceful Error Handling: Prevent one failing task from breaking the entire workflow.

Exercise: Optimize a Data Pipeline

Task:

1. Fetch data from three APIs.
2. Clean the data concurrently.
3. Generate a report summarizing the results.
4. Measure and compare performance with sequential execution.

6.4 Security, Privacy, and Ethical AI Practices

As AI continues to evolve and become more integrated into critical systems, addressing security, privacy, and ethical concerns is no longer optional—it's essential. AI systems have the power to influence decision-making, process sensitive data, and interact directly with users. If these systems are not built and managed responsibly, they can introduce significant risks, including data breaches, biased outcomes, and unintended harm.

Why AI Security Matters

AI systems often interact with sensitive data and external services, making them attractive targets for malicious actors. Poor security practices can result in:

- Data breaches exposing personal or business information.
- Model poisoning where attackers manipulate training data to alter model behavior.
- Adversarial attacks that trick models into making incorrect decisions.
- Unauthorized access to APIs or systems.

Common AI Security Threats

1. Adversarial Attacks: Small, imperceptible changes to input data can trick AI models into making wrong decisions.
2. Data Poisoning: Corrupting training data to influence model predictions.
3. Model Inversion: Attackers reverse-engineer models to extract sensitive training data.
4. API Abuse: Exploiting AI APIs with malicious inputs or excessive requests.

Best Practices for Securing AI Systems

- Input Validation: Sanitize and validate all user inputs to prevent injection attacks.
- Rate Limiting: Restrict the number of API calls to prevent abuse.
- Encryption: Encrypt sensitive data during storage and transmission.
- Access Control: Implement role-based access controls to limit system access.
- Monitoring and Logging: Continuously monitor system activity and log suspicious behavior.

Example: Securing API Keys in Python

Hardcoding sensitive credentials like API keys is risky. A secure approach is to load them from environment variables.

```python
import os

from dotenv import load_dotenv


# Load environment variables from .env file

load_dotenv()
```

```python
# Securely load the API key

API_KEY = os.getenv("API_KEY")


def secure_api_call():

    if not API_KEY:

        return "Error: API key not found."

    # Simulate API call

    return "API call successful with secured key."


print(secure_api_call())
```

Explanation:

- The API key is stored securely in a .env file, preventing accidental exposure in code repositories.
- Always use environment variables for sensitive information.

Why Privacy Matters

AI systems often process vast amounts of personal and sensitive data. Mishandling this data can lead to:

- Violations of privacy laws like GDPR and CCPA.
- Loss of user trust.
- Legal and financial consequences.

Key Privacy Principles

1. Data Minimization: Collect only the data necessary for the task.
2. Transparency: Inform users about data collection and how it's used.
3. User Consent: Obtain clear consent before collecting or processing personal data.
4. Right to Erasure: Allow users to request the deletion of their data.

Techniques for Privacy Protection

- Data Anonymization: Remove identifiable information from datasets.
- Differential Privacy: Introduce noise into data to prevent individual identification.
- Federated Learning: Train models on local devices without sharing raw data.

Example: Data Anonymization

Here's how to anonymize personal data in a dataset.

```
import pandas as pd



# Sample data

data = {

    'Name': ['Alice', 'Bob', 'Charlie'],

    'Email': ['alice@example.com',
'bob@example.com', 'charlie@example.com'],

    'Purchase': [200, 150, 300]

}
```

```
df = pd.DataFrame(data)


# Anonymize sensitive columns

df['Name'] = 'User_' + (df.index + 1).astype(str)

df['Email'] = 'hidden@example.com'


print(df)
```

Expected Output:

	Name	Email	Purchase
0	User_1	hidden@example.com	200
1	User_2	hidden@example.com	150
2	User_3	hidden@example.com	300

Explanation:

- Personally identifiable information (PII) is replaced with anonymized labels.
- This allows data analysis while protecting user privacy.

Why Ethics in AI is Critical

AI systems can make decisions that significantly impact people's lives. If not carefully designed, these systems can:

- Amplify biases.
- Make unfair decisions.

- Cause unintended harm.

Core Ethical AI Principles

1. Fairness: AI should treat all individuals and groups fairly without bias.
2. Accountability: Developers must be responsible for how AI systems behave.
3. Transparency: Systems should be explainable and understandable.
4. Inclusivity: AI should be designed to serve diverse populations.
5. Beneficence: AI must prioritize human well-being.

Bias in AI Models

AI models trained on biased data can produce biased outcomes. For example:

- A loan approval model trained on biased data may unfairly deny loans to certain demographics.
- A facial recognition system may perform poorly on specific ethnic groups due to unbalanced training data.

Detecting and Mitigating Bias

1. Audit Training Data: Check for imbalance in datasets.
2. Fairness Metrics: Use tools like Demographic Parity or Equal Opportunity to measure fairness.
3. Bias Mitigation: Apply techniques like re-weighting or data augmentation.

Example: Detecting Bias in a Dataset

Let's check for gender imbalance in a hiring dataset.

```
# Sample hiring dataset
```

```
data = {

    'Gender': ['Male', 'Female', 'Male', 'Male',
'Female'],

    'Hired': [1, 0, 1, 1, 0]

}



df = pd.DataFrame(data)



# Check hiring rates by gender

hiring_rates =
df.groupby('Gender')['Hired'].mean()

print(hiring_rates)
```

Expected Output:

Gender

Female   0.0

Male   1.0

Name: Hired, dtype: float64

Explanation:

- Male applicants have a 100% hiring rate, while female applicants have 0%.
- This reveals a clear bias in the hiring decisions.

Best Practices for Ethical AI

1. Bias Auditing: Regularly test AI models for bias and discrimination.
2. Explainability: Use interpretable models or tools to explain AI decisions.
3. Human Oversight: Keep humans in the loop for critical decisions.
4. Data Governance: Set policies for data collection, storage, and use.
5. Regular Updates: Continuously improve models with diverse and representative data.

Exercise: Build a Privacy-First AI Assistant

Task:

1. Create a chatbot that only stores non-personal data.
2. Anonymize any sensitive user input.
3. Implement a feature to delete user data on request.

6.5 Performance Tuning and Resource Management

As AI systems grow more complex and handle larger datasets, performance tuning and efficient resource management become critical for ensuring that these systems are both responsive and scalable. Without proper optimization, even the most sophisticated AI solutions can become slow, resource-hungry, and costly to maintain.

Why Performance Tuning and Resource Management Matter

1. Scalability: Optimized systems can handle increased workloads without needing proportionally more resources.

2. Cost Efficiency: Efficient resource use reduces infrastructure and cloud service costs.

3. Speed and Responsiveness: Faster processing times improve user experience and system responsiveness.

4. Stability: Balanced resource allocation prevents system crashes and downtime under heavy load.

Key Concepts in Performance Tuning

1. Bottleneck Identification: Detects slow or resource-heavy parts of the system.
2. Efficient Algorithms: Use optimized algorithms and data structures.
3. Parallelism and Concurrency: Execute tasks in parallel to reduce latency.
4. Caching: Store frequently used data to avoid redundant computation.
5. Resource Monitoring: Continuously track system resource usage.

Identifying Bottlenecks

Before optimizing, you must identify which parts of your system are slowing it down. Python's cProfile module is a useful tool for profiling code.

Example: Using cProfile to Detect Slow Functions

```
import cProfile


def slow_function():

    total = 0
```

```
    for i in range(10_000_000):

        total += i

    return total


def fast_function():

    return sum(range(10_000_000))



# Profile both functions

cProfile.run('slow_function()')

cProfile.run('fast_function()')
```

Explanation:

- cProfile will show you how much time each function takes to execute.
- Replace inefficient loops with optimized functions like Python's built-in sum().

Optimizing Data Processing

1. Batch Processing: Processing data in batches is more efficient than handling each item individually.

Example: Batch Processing vs. Sequential Processing

```
import time



# Sequential processing
```

```python
def sequential_processing(data):

    for item in data:

        time.sleep(0.1)   # Simulate a
time-consuming task

    return "Sequential Processing Done"


# Batch processing

def batch_processing(data, batch_size):

    for i in range(0, len(data), batch_size):

        time.sleep(0.1)   # Simulate processing

    return "Batch Processing Done"


# Test the functions

data = list(range(100))


start = time.time()

sequential_processing(data)

print(f"Sequential: {time.time() - start:.2f}
seconds")


start = time.time()
```

```
batch_processing(data, batch_size=10)

print(f"Batch: {time.time() - start:.2f}
seconds")
```

Expected Output:

Sequential: 10.01 seconds

Batch: 1.01 seconds

Explanation:

- Batch processing groups tasks, reducing overhead and speeding up execution.

2. Caching for Repeated Computations: Repeatedly performing the same computation wastes resources. Caching can store results of expensive operations.

Example: Using functools.lru_cache for Caching

```
from functools import lru_cache

import time


# Without caching

def slow_square(n):

    time.sleep(1)   # Simulate expensive
computation

    return n * n
```

```
# With caching

@lru_cache(maxsize=None)

def cached_square(n):

    time.sleep(1)

    return n * n


start = time.time()

print(slow_square(10))   # Takes 1 second

print(slow_square(10))   # Takes 1 second

print(f"Without cache: {time.time() - start:.2f}
seconds")


start = time.time()

print(cached_square(10))   # Takes 1 second

print(cached_square(10))   # Instant

print(f"With cache: {time.time() - start:.2f}
seconds")
```

Expected Output:

100

100

Without cache: 2.00 seconds

100

100

With cache: 1.00 seconds

Explanation:

- The cached version saves the result and avoids redundant computation.

Parallel and Asynchronous Processing

Parallel and asynchronous programming help maximize CPU and I/O resource usage.

1. Parallel Processing with multiprocessing

For CPU-intensive tasks, use Python's multiprocessing to distribute work across cores.

```
from multiprocessing import Pool


def compute_square(n):

    return n * n


numbers = list(range(1, 10_001))


# Parallel processing

with Pool() as pool:

    results = pool.map(compute_square, numbers)
```

```
print("Parallel processing completed.")
```

Explanation:

- Distributes work across multiple CPU cores, speeding up heavy computations.

2. Asynchronous Processing with asyncio

For I/O-bound tasks (e.g., API calls), asynchronous processing prevents blocking.

```
import asyncio

import aiohttp


async def fetch_url(session, url):

    async with session.get(url) as response:

        return await response.text()


async def main():

    urls = [


"https://jsonplaceholder.typicode.com/posts/1",


"https://jsonplaceholder.typicode.com/posts/2"

    ]
```

```
    async with aiohttp.ClientSession() as
session:

        tasks = [fetch_url(session, url) for url
in urls]

        responses = await asyncio.gather(*tasks)

        for res in responses:

            print(res[:100])   # Print first 100
characters


asyncio.run(main())
```

Explanation:

- Runs API requests simultaneously, reducing overall wait time.

Resource Monitoring and Management

Monitoring system resources ensures optimal performance and prevents overload.

1. Monitoring with psutil

```
The psutil library tracks CPU, memory, and disk
usage.

import psutil


def monitor_resources():

    cpu_usage = psutil.cpu_percent(interval=1)
```

```
memory_info = psutil.virtual_memory()


print(f"CPU Usage: {cpu_usage}%")

print(f"Memory Usage:
{memory_info.percent}%")



monitor_resources()
```

Explanation:

- Continuously monitoring resource usage helps prevent system overload.

Best Practices for Performance Tuning

1. Profile Before Optimizing: Use tools like cProfile to find actual bottlenecks.
2. Cache Repetitive Work: Use caching to avoid redundant processing.
3. Batch and Stream Data: Process large datasets in manageable batches.
4. Parallelize Where Appropriate: Use multiprocessing or asyncio for heavy workloads.
5. Monitor in Production: Implement resource monitoring to catch issues early.
6. Limit Resource Usage: Use throttling and rate limits to prevent overuse.

Exercise: Optimize a Data Processing Pipeline

Task:

1. Create a script that reads a large dataset.

2. Optimize data loading using batch processing.
3. Implement caching for repetitive computations.
4. Monitor CPU and memory usage.

Chapter 7: Deploying and Scaling AI Workflows

Developing intelligent AI workflows is only part of the journey. For these systems to provide real-world value, they must be effectively deployed and scaled to handle production-level demands. Deployment is about moving your AI model or workflow from development to a live environment, while scaling ensures that the system can handle growing workloads without sacrificing performance or reliability.

7.1 Deployment Strategies for AI Workflows

Building powerful AI models is only half the job. To deliver real-world value, these models must be effectively deployed in production environments. Deployment ensures that your AI solutions are accessible, reliable, and scalable for end users. However, deploying AI workflows comes with its own challenges, such as performance optimization, scalability, reliability, and security.

Why Deployment Strategies Matter

Deploying AI workflows requires careful planning because:

- AI models are resource-intensive. They often require powerful compute resources (CPU/GPU).
- AI workflows can be complex. They involve data preprocessing, model inference, and integration with other systems.
- User demand can fluctuate. Systems must handle varying loads smoothly.

- Security and compliance must be maintained, especially when dealing with sensitive data.

A thoughtful deployment strategy ensures that the AI model remains efficient, secure, and scalable.

Types of Deployment Strategies

1. Batch Deployment: Batch deployment processes large datasets in chunks at scheduled intervals. It's best for tasks that don't need real-time results.

Use Cases:

- Financial report generation.
- Monthly customer segmentation analysis.
- Training recommendation systems overnight.

Pros:

- Efficient for processing large datasets.
- Lower resource usage due to off-peak execution.

Cons:

- Not suitable for real-time applications.

Example: Generating a daily sales report.

```python
import pandas as pd


def generate_daily_report():

    data = pd.read_csv('sales_data.csv')

    daily_sales =
data.groupby('date')['revenue'].sum()
```

```
daily_sales.to_csv('daily_report.csv')

print("Daily sales report generated.")
```

```
generate_daily_report()
```

Explanation:

- This script processes data once per day.
- The output is a summarized report, suitable for batch processing.

2. Online (Real-Time) Deployment: The model is hosted as a live service, providing instant predictions to users or systems.

Use Cases:

- Chatbots responding to user queries.
- Fraud detection in banking.
- Real-time recommendation engines.

Pros:

- Provides immediate feedback.
- Ideal for dynamic and interactive applications.

Cons:

- Requires more robust infrastructure to handle peak loads.
- More complex to manage and scale.

Example: Deploying a model with **Flask** for real-time inference.

```
from flask import Flask, request, jsonify

import joblib
```

```python
# Load the trained model

model = joblib.load("model.pkl")


app = Flask(__name__)


@app.route('/predict', methods=['POST'])

def predict():

    data = request.get_json(force=True)

    prediction =
model.predict([data['features']])

    return jsonify({'prediction':
prediction.tolist()})


if __name__ == '__main__':

    app.run(debug=True)
```

Explanation:

- The model is exposed via an API, handling real-time predictions.
- A client can send feature data and instantly receive predictions.

3. Streaming Deployment: Handles continuous data streams and makes decisions in real-time.

Use Cases:

- Stock market trading bots.
- IoT devices sending telemetry data.
- Real-time video or image processing.

Pros:

- Designed for real-time, high-throughput systems.
- Ideal for continuous data flows.

Cons:

- Requires complex infrastructure.
- Difficult to manage state across streams.

Example: Stream processing with Python using Kafka.

```
from kafka import KafkaConsumer
```

```
# Consume real-time data from Kafka topic

consumer = KafkaConsumer('sensor-data',
bootstrap_servers='localhost:9092')
```

```
for message in consumer:

    print(f"Received data:
{message.value.decode()}")
```

Explanation:

- Continuously listens to a Kafka topic for real-time data.
- Ideal for IoT and sensor data processing.

4. Serverless Deployment: Deploy models using serverless platforms where the cloud provider manages the infrastructure.

Use Cases:

- Low-traffic applications.
- Event-driven tasks (e.g., trigger-based predictions).
- Scalable microservices.

Pros:

- Automatically scales with demand.
- Pay only for what you use.
- No server management required.

Cons:

- Cold start latency.
- Resource limitations (memory, execution time).

Example: Deploying a model on **AWS Lambda**

```python
import json

import joblib


# Load model once during cold start

model = joblib.load('/opt/ml/model.pkl')


def lambda_handler(event, context):

    data = json.loads(event['body'])
```

```
    prediction =
model.predict([data['features']])

    return {

        'statusCode': 200,

        'body': json.dumps({'prediction':
prediction.tolist()})

    }
```

Explanation:

- The function automatically scales to handle incoming requests.
- No server management or provisioning is needed.

5. Containerized Deployment with Docker: Deploying the entire AI workflow in a Docker container for portability and scalability.

Use Cases:

- Microservice architectures.
- Scalable AI workflows with Kubernetes.

Pros:

- Easy to deploy and replicate across environments.
- Isolated and consistent execution.

Cons:

- Requires Docker knowledge.
- Adds container orchestration complexity for scaling.

Dockerfile Example:

```
FROM python:3.8
```

```
WORKDIR /app


COPY requirements.txt .

RUN pip install -r requirements.txt


COPY . .


CMD ["python", "app.py"]
```

Explanation:

- This Dockerfile packages the AI workflow into a portable container.
- Easy to deploy on any system with Docker.

Choosing the Right Deployment Strategy

Criteria	Batch	Online	Stream ing	Serverl ess	Contai nerized
Real-Ti me Predict ions	No	Yes	Yes	Yes	Yes

Scalability	Low	High	High	Auto-scaled	High (with orchestration)
Cost Efficiency	High (low cost)	Medium-High	High	High	Medium
Maintenance Effort	Low	High	High	Low	Medium

Best Practices for Deploying AI Workflows

1. Automate Deployments: Use CI/CD pipelines for faster and safer deployments.
2. Containerize Workflows: Use Docker/Kubernetes for scalable, portable deployments.
3. Monitor Performance: Continuously track system metrics and model drift.
4. Ensure Security: Protect APIs with authentication and encrypt sensitive data.
5. Implement Auto-Scaling: Prepare for traffic spikes with horizontal scaling.
6. Version Models: Keep track of different model versions for easy rollbacks.

Exercise: Deploy a Sentiment Analysis Model

Task:

1. Train a sentiment analysis model (positive/negative review classification).
2. Deploy the model using Flask or FastAPI.
3. Expose an API for real-time predictions.

Choosing the right deployment strategy is critical for ensuring your AI workflow is efficient, scalable, and accessible. Whether you need batch processing, real-time predictions, or scalable microservices, aligning the deployment approach with your use case ensures optimal performance. By leveraging best practices and tools, you can transition from development to production seamlessly and effectively.

7.2 Scaling Workflows for High Performance

Building an AI workflow that functions well in development is one thing, but ensuring it performs efficiently under real-world conditions with growing demands is another challenge entirely. Scaling workflows for high performance is about designing systems that can handle increased workloads, higher user demands, and larger datasets without compromising speed, reliability, or accuracy.

Why Scaling is Critical for AI Workflows

AI workflows often involve processing vast amounts of data, serving predictions in real-time, and interacting with multiple services. Without proper scaling:

- Performance slows down under heavy load.
- Systems crash due to resource exhaustion.
- User experience deteriorates, leading to lost business.

Scaling ensures that the system can:

- Handle growing user demand.
- Maintain high availability and reliability.
- Optimize resource usage and reduce operational costs.

Types of Scaling

1. Vertical Scaling (Scaling Up): Increasing the capacity of a single machine by adding more CPU, RAM, or storage.

Pros:

- Easier to implement.
- No need to redesign the architecture.

Cons:

- Limited by hardware capacity.
- Downtime is often required for upgrades.

Use Case:
  Useful for small-scale applications that don't need complex infrastructure.

2. Horizontal Scaling (Scaling Out): Adding more machines or instances to distribute workloads.

Pros:

- High availability (redundancy across multiple instances).
- No hardware limits—can scale infinitely with cloud resources.

Cons:

- Requires load balancers and more complex architecture.
- Increased management overhead.

Use Case:
Ideal for web applications, AI inference APIs, and large-scale data processing.

Scaling Techniques

1. Load Balancing: Distributes incoming requests across multiple servers to ensure no single machine is overloaded.

How it Works:
A load balancer sits between the client and backend servers. It routes traffic based on rules like server load, response time, or health checks.

Common Tools:

- Nginx
- HAProxy
- Cloud Load Balancers (AWS ELB, Azure Load Balancer)

Example: Load Balancing with Nginx

Step 1: Install Nginx.

```
sudo apt update

sudo apt install nginx
```

Step 2: Configure Nginx as a load balancer.

```
http {

    upstream backend {

        server 127.0.0.1:8001;

        server 127.0.0.1:8002;
```

```
        }


    server {

        listen 80;


        location / {

            proxy_pass http://backend;

        }

    }

}
```

Explanation:

- Requests are distributed between two backend servers (8001 and 8002).
- This prevents any single server from becoming a bottleneck.

2. Autoscaling: Automatically adjusts the number of running instances based on demand.

How it Works:

Autoscaling monitors metrics like CPU usage or incoming traffic and scales resources up or down accordingly.

Common Tools:

- AWS Auto Scaling Groups
- Google Cloud Autoscaler

- Azure VM Scale Sets

Example: Autoscaling with AWS Lambda

AWS Lambda automatically scales without any configuration. Here's how to deploy a serverless AI function.

```python
import json

import joblib


# Load the trained model

model = joblib.load('/opt/ml/model.pkl')


def lambda_handler(event, context):

    data = json.loads(event['body'])

    prediction =
model.predict([data['features']])

    return {

        'statusCode': 200,

        'body': json.dumps({'prediction':
prediction.tolist()})

    }
```

Explanation:

- AWS Lambda automatically scales to handle concurrent requests.

- You only pay for what you use, with no manual scaling.

3. Distributed Processing: Breaks large datasets into smaller parts and processes them across multiple machines in parallel.

Common Tools:

- Apache Spark for distributed data processing.
- Dask for parallel computing in Python.
- Ray for scalable AI and ML workloads.

Example: Distributed Data Processing with Dask

```
import dask.array as da
```

```
# Create a large array with Dask

x = da.random.random((10000, 10000),
chunks=(1000, 1000))
```

```
# Perform parallel computation

result = x.mean().compute()
```

```
print(f"Mean of large array: {result}")
```

Explanation:

- Dask splits the computation into chunks and runs them in parallel.
- This drastically reduces computation time for large datasets.

Optimizing AI Models for Scalability

1. Model Quantization

Reduces model size by using lower precision (e.g., converting 32-bit floats to 8-bit integers) without significantly impacting accuracy.

Tools:

- TensorFlow Lite
- PyTorch Quantization

2. Model Pruning

Removes unnecessary neurons or parameters from the model to reduce complexity.

Tools:

- TensorFlow Model Optimization Toolkit
- PyTorch Pruning APIs

3. Batch Inference

Processes multiple inputs at once instead of one-by-one, improving throughput.

Example: Batch Prediction

```
import numpy as np


def batch_predict(model, data, batch_size=32):

    predictions = []

    for i in range(0, len(data), batch_size):
```

```
    batch = data[i:i + batch_size]

    predictions.extend(model.predict(batch))

  return predictions
```

Explanation:

- The function processes data in batches, reducing the number of inference calls.
- This improves efficiency for large datasets.

Best Practices for Scaling AI Workflows

1. Start with Horizontal Scaling: Add more servers to handle increasing load.
2. Implement Load Balancing: Distribute workloads evenly across servers.
3. Use Autoscaling: Automate scaling based on real-time demand.
4. Optimize Models: Apply quantization, pruning, and batch processing.
5. Monitor Continuously: Use tools like Prometheus or CloudWatch to track performance.
6. Decouple Components: Use microservices to isolate workloads for independent scaling.
7. Cache Frequently Used Data: Use Redis or Memcached to reduce redundant processing.

Exercise: Implement a Scalable Prediction API

Task:

1. Containerize a prediction API using Docker.
2. Deploy multiple instances of the API.
3. Configure Nginx as a load balancer to distribute requests.

7.3 Monitoring and Maintaining Deployed Systems

Deploying an AI system is a significant milestone, but the real challenge begins once it's live. Monitoring and maintaining deployed systems is essential to ensure that your AI workflows remain reliable, efficient, and secure. Without continuous monitoring and proactive maintenance, even the best-designed systems can degrade over time, leading to poor performance, unexpected failures, and user dissatisfaction.

Why Monitoring and Maintenance Are Crucial

1. Detecting and Resolving Issues Early: Monitoring helps catch problems before they escalate, minimizing downtime and performance issues.

2. Maintain System Performance: Performance can degrade due to increased workloads, inefficient resource use, or unexpected errors.

3. Ensure Security and Compliance: Continuous monitoring protects systems against security threats and helps maintain compliance with data protection laws.

4. Manage Model Accuracy (Model Drift): AI models can lose accuracy over time due to changing data patterns (concept drift). Monitoring ensures models remain effective.

Key Components to Monitor

1. System Performance Metrics

- CPU and Memory Usage: Overuse can slow down or crash systems.

- Disk I/O and Network Latency: Bottlenecks in storage and network can degrade performance.
- Response Times: Measures how quickly the system responds to user requests.
- Error Rates: Frequency of failed requests or exceptions.

2. Model Performance Metrics

- Prediction Accuracy: Monitors how well the model performs on live data.
- Input/Output Distribution: Detects data drift when input data patterns change.
- Model Drift: Monitors gradual performance degradation due to outdated models.
- Inference Latency: Measures how fast the model generates predictions.

3. Application Health Metrics

- Uptime/Downtime: Tracks system availability.
- API Health: Checks whether APIs are responsive.
- Database Health: Monitors database connections and query performance.

Monitoring Tools and Techniques

1. Logging: Logs record detailed information about system behavior, errors, and user interactions. They're crucial for debugging and understanding issues.

Popular Tools:

- Python's logging module
- ELK Stack (Elasticsearch, Logstash, Kibana)
- Fluentd

Example: Logging in Python

```python
import logging

# Configure logging

logging.basicConfig(filename='app.log',
level=logging.INFO)


def predict(data):
    try:
        # Simulate prediction
        if data is None:
            raise ValueError("Invalid data")
        result = data * 2
        logging.info(f"Prediction successful:
{result}")
        return result
    except Exception as e:
        logging.error(f"Prediction failed: {e}")
        return None


predict(5)
predict(None)
```

Explanation:

- Successful predictions are logged as INFO.
- Errors are logged as ERROR for easier troubleshooting.

2. Metrics Monitoring: Metrics provide real-time insights into system and model performance.

Popular Tools:

- Prometheus (metrics collection)
- Grafana (visualization)
- CloudWatch (AWS monitoring)

Example: Exposing Metrics with Prometheus

```python
from prometheus_client import start_http_server, Summary

import random

import time



# Create a metric to track time spent

REQUEST_TIME =
Summary('request_processing_seconds', 'Time spent processing request')



@REQUEST_TIME.time()

def process_request():

    time.sleep(random.random())
```

```
if __name__ == "__main__":

    # Start Prometheus metrics server

    start_http_server(8000)

    while True:

        process_request()
```

Explanation:

- This script tracks the time it takes to process a request.
- Prometheus can scrape this data, and Grafana can visualize it.

3. Health Checks: Health checks help verify if services are running correctly.

Popular Tools:

- Kubernetes Readiness/Liveness Probes
- Load Balancers with health check configurations

Example: Flask Health Check Endpoint

```
from flask import Flask, jsonify


app = Flask(__name__)


@app.route('/health', methods=['GET'])

def health_check():
```

```python
# Simulate a health check

return jsonify(status="healthy"), 200


if __name__ == "__main__":

    app.run(port=5000)
```

Explanation:

- External services can ping /health to verify if the app is running.
- A 200 OK response means the service is healthy.

4. Alerting: Automated alerts notify teams of issues in real-time.

Popular Tools:

- Prometheus Alertmanager
- PagerDuty
- Slack integrations

Example: Setting Up Prometheus Alert

```yaml
groups:

  - name: CPU_Alerts

    rules:

      - alert: HighCPUUsage

        expr: process_cpu_seconds_total > 80

        for: 5m

        labels:
```

```
severity: critical

annotations:

  summary: "High CPU usage detected"
```

Explanation:

- If CPU usage exceeds 80% for more than 5 minutes, an alert is triggered.
- This alert can be sent to **Slack, email, or any** incident response system.

Maintaining Deployed AI Systems

1. Handling Model Drift: Model drift occurs when a model's performance degrades due to changes in the underlying data.

Strategies to Mitigate Drift:

- Data Monitoring: Track changes in input data distribution.
- Performance Testing: Regularly validate model predictions.
- Scheduled Retraining: Automate model retraining with new data.

2. Updating Models in Production: Deploy updated models without disrupting the service.

Strategies:

- Canary Deployment: Gradually roll out the new model to a small user group.
- A/B Testing: Deploy two models and compare their performance.
- Blue-Green Deployment: Run the old and new versions side-by-side and switch traffic gradually.

Example: Canary Deployment

1. Deploy Model V2 to 10% of traffic.
2. Monitor performance metrics.
3. If stable, gradually increase traffic to 100%.

3. Automating Maintenance: Automating tasks reduces human error and speeds up routine operations.

Common Maintenance Automations:

- Backup and Recovery: Regular data backups and disaster recovery plans.
- Autoscaling: Adjust compute resources automatically.
- Scheduled Cleanups: Clear logs and temporary files to free up storage.

Example: Automated Log Rotation

```
# Rotate logs daily and keep 7 backups

/var/log/app.log {

    daily

    rotate 7

    compress

    missingok

    notifempty

}
```

Explanation:

- This logrotate configuration automatically manages log files to prevent disk overload.

Best Practices for Monitoring and Maintenance

1. Set Clear SLAs: Define acceptable performance and uptime metrics.
2. Automate Health Checks: Implement health checks at every layer (API, database, services).
3. Use Redundancy: Deploy redundant servers for high availability.
4. Continuously Monitor Models: Watch for data drift and performance degradation.
5. Implement Role-Based Access: Limit who can make changes to the system.
6. Document Everything: Keep detailed documentation for monitoring tools and incident responses.
7. Regular Test Failures: Simulate outages to test system resilience.

Exercise: Implement End-to-End Monitoring

Task:

1. Deploy an AI API using Flask.
2. Add a health check endpoint.
3. Expose performance metrics using Prometheus.
4. Set up an alert for high CPU usage.

7.4 Integrating with Cloud and Edge Infrastructure

Deploying AI systems in production requires more than just a functional model—it demands a robust infrastructure that can support scalability, speed, and reliability. **Cloud** and **Edge Computing** are two critical infrastructures that enable AI systems to meet these demands effectively. Integrating AI workflows with these infrastructures allows for seamless scalability, low-latency responses, and efficient resource management.

Why Cloud and Edge Integration Matters

Cloud Infrastructure

- Provides on-demand scalability.
- Offers powerful computing resources (CPU, GPU, TPU).
- Ideal for training large models and handling heavy workloads.

Edge Infrastructure

- Brings computation closer to the data source (e.g., IoT devices, mobile phones).
- Reduces latency and improves response times.
- Ideal for real-time, privacy-sensitive, or offline applications.

Hybrid Approach

Combining both cloud and edge infrastructures enables AI systems to leverage the scalability of the cloud with the speed and proximity of the edge.

Cloud Integration for AI Workflows

Popular Cloud Providers for AI

1. **Amazon Web Services (AWS)**
   - Services: SageMaker, Lambda, EC2, S3
2. **Google Cloud Platform (GCP)**
   - Services: AI Platform, Cloud Functions, Compute Engine
3. **Microsoft Azure**
   - Services: Azure ML, Functions, Virtual Machines

Deploying AI Models with AWS SageMaker

AWS SageMaker is a fully managed service that helps you train, deploy, and scale machine learning models.

Step 1: Install Required Libraries

```
pip install sagemaker boto3
```

Step 2: Deploy a Model to SageMaker

```
import sagemaker

from sagemaker.sklearn.model import SKLearnModel


# Initialize SageMaker session

sagemaker_session = sagemaker.Session()

role = 'arn:aws:iam::123456789012:role/SageMakerRole'


# Define the model

model = SKLearnModel(

    model_data='s3://my-bucket/model.tar.gz',

    role=role,

    entry_point='predict.py',

    framework_version='0.23-1'

)
```

```
# Deploy the model

predictor = model.deploy(

    instance_type='ml.m5.large',

    initial_instance_count=1

)


# Test the deployment

response = predictor.predict([1.5, 2.3, 3.1])

print(response)
```

Explanation:

- S3 stores the model artifact.
- SageMaker handles deployment and scaling.
- The model is now live and accessible via API for predictions.

Serverless Deployment with Google Cloud Functions

Serverless deployment allows running AI workflows without managing servers.

Step 1: Install Google Cloud CLI

gcloud init

Step 2: Deploy a Model as a Cloud Function

```
import json

import joblib
```

```
# Load the model

model = joblib.load('model.pkl')


def predict(request):

    request_json = request.get_json()

    features = request_json['features']

    prediction = model.predict([features])

    return json.dumps({'prediction':
prediction.tolist()})
```

Deploy the function:

```
gcloud functions deploy predict \

  --runtime python39 \

  --trigger-http \

  --allow-unauthenticated
```

Explanation:

- This function scales automatically with demand.
- It serves predictions via an HTTP endpoint without server management.

Edge Integration for AI Workflows

Edge computing moves computation closer to data sources like IoT devices, cameras, or mobile devices. This reduces latency and lowers reliance on internet connectivity.

Use Cases for Edge Deployment

- Smart Cameras: Real-time object detection on security cameras.
- IoT Devices: Predictive maintenance in manufacturing equipment.
- Autonomous Vehicles: Real-time sensor data processing for navigation.
- Healthcare Devices: On-device patient monitoring and diagnosis.

Deploying AI Models on Edge Devices with TensorFlow Lite

TensorFlow Lite allows deploying lightweight models on edge devices.

Step 1: Convert a Model to TensorFlow Lite

```
import tensorflow as tf



# Load a pre-trained model

model = tf.keras.models.load_model('model.h5')



# Convert to TensorFlow Lite format

converter =
tf.lite.TFLiteConverter.from_keras_model(model)

tflite_model = converter.convert()



# Save the model

with open('model.tflite', 'wb') as f:
```

```
    f.write(tflite_model)
```

Step 2: Run Inference on a Raspberry Pi

```
import tensorflow as tf

import numpy as np


# Load the TFLite model

interpreter =
tf.lite.Interpreter(model_path="model.tflite")

interpreter.allocate_tensors()


# Get input and output tensors

input_details = interpreter.get_input_details()

output_details = interpreter.get_output_details()


# Prepare input data

input_data = np.array([[1.5, 2.3, 3.1]],
dtype=np.float32)


# Run inference

interpreter.set_tensor(input_details[0]['index'],
input_data)

interpreter.invoke()
```

```
output_data =
interpreter.get_tensor(output_details[0]['index']
)
```

```
print(f"Prediction: {output_data}")
```

Explanation:

- The model is optimized and deployed to a lightweight device (e.g., Raspberry Pi).
- Inference runs directly on the device, minimizing latency.

Hybrid Deployment: Cloud + Edge

Why Use a Hybrid Approach?

- Cloud for model training and heavy computation.
- Edge for real-time inference and low-latency tasks.

Example Workflow:

1. Train a large model in the cloud (AWS/GCP).
2. Optimize and convert the model for edge deployment.
3. Deploy the model to IoT devices or mobile apps for real-time predictions.

Best Practices for Integration

1. Optimize Models for Deployment: Use quantization and pruning to reduce model size.
2. Secure Data Transmission: Encrypt data between cloud and edge devices.
3. Automate Deployment: Use CI/CD pipelines for seamless updates.
4. Monitor Both Cloud and Edge: Implement monitoring for performance and security.

5. Balance Load: Offload intensive tasks to the cloud, lightweight tasks to the edge.
6. Implement Failover Strategies: Ensure edge devices can operate offline if cloud services fail.

Exercise: End-to-End Deployment

Task:

1. Train a model in the cloud (AWS or GCP).
2. Convert the model for edge deployment (TensorFlow Lite).
3. Deploy the model to a Raspberry Pi or mobile device for real-time inference.

7.5 Continuous Improvement and Updates

Deploying an AI system is not the final step in its lifecycle. To maintain optimal performance, relevance, and reliability, continuous improvement and regular updates are essential. AI models are highly sensitive to changes in data, user behavior, and market dynamics. Without consistent monitoring, maintenance, and updates, even the most accurate models will eventually degrade in performance due to factors like model drift, data shifts, or changing user needs.

Why Continuous Improvement Matters

1. Model Drift: Model performance can degrade over time as data patterns shift, leading to concept drift and data drift. Continuous updates help mitigate this.

2. Changing Business Needs: Market trends and user expectations evolve, requiring models to adapt to new goals and behaviors.

3. Technological Advancements: New algorithms, libraries, or hardware improvements can provide opportunities to optimize performance.

4. Regulatory Compliance: AI models must stay compliant with data privacy laws and industry regulations, which often change over time.

Key Components of Continuous Improvement

1. Monitoring and Feedback Loops

- Model Performance Monitoring: Track real-world model performance using key metrics (accuracy, precision, recall).
- User Feedback Integration: Incorporate user feedback to identify areas for improvement.
- Error Analysis: Identify and analyze mispredictions to refine the model.

2. Automated Retraining Pipelines

- Automate model retraining using newly collected data.
- Implement CI/CD pipelines for safe, efficient updates.

3. A/B Testing and Canary Releases

- Gradually roll out new models to a subset of users to compare performance.
- Reduce risk when deploying updated models.

4. Version Control for Models

- Use model versioning to track changes and easily roll back if needed.

Implementing Continuous Improvement

1. Monitoring Model Performance

Let's begin by monitoring model accuracy in production.

Example: Real-Time Model Monitoring

```python
import pandas as pd

from sklearn.metrics import accuracy_score


# Simulated real-time predictions

actual = pd.Series([1, 0, 1, 1, 0, 0, 1])

predicted = pd.Series([1, 0, 0, 1, 0, 1, 1])


# Monitor model accuracy

def monitor_model_performance(actual, predicted):

    accuracy = accuracy_score(actual, predicted)

    if accuracy < 0.8:

        print(f"Warning: Model accuracy dropped
to {accuracy:.2f}")

    else:

        print(f"Model running fine with accuracy:
{accuracy:.2f}")


monitor_model_performance(actual, predicted)
```

Explanation:

- This function continuously checks model performance.
- If accuracy drops below a threshold, it flags the issue.

2. Automating Model Retraining

Automating retraining is critical for keeping models relevant.

Example: Scheduled Model Retraining

```
import pandas as pd

from sklearn.linear_model import
LogisticRegression

import joblib


def retrain_model():

    # Load new data

    data = pd.read_csv('new_training_data.csv')

    X, y = data.drop('label', axis=1),
data['label']


    # Retrain model

    model = LogisticRegression()

    model.fit(X, y)


    # Save updated model
```

```
joblib.dump(model, 'updated_model.pkl')

print("Model retrained and saved.")



# Schedule retraining (e.g., every week using a
scheduler)

retrain_model()
```

Explanation:

- This script retrains a model with new data.
- Can be automated using schedulers like **cron** or cloud workflows.

3. Version Control for Models

Model versioning allows teams to track changes and manage updates.

Example: Model Versioning with MLflow

```
import mlflow

import mlflow.sklearn

from sklearn.linear_model import
LogisticRegression



# Enable MLflow tracking

mlflow.set_tracking_uri("http://localhost:5000")



def log_model():
```

```
model = LogisticRegression()

model.fit([[0, 0], [1, 1]], [0, 1])


with mlflow.start_run():

    mlflow.sklearn.log_model(model,
"logistic_regression_model")

    mlflow.log_param("model_type", "Logistic
Regression")

    mlflow.log_metric("accuracy", 0.95)

    print("Model version logged.")


log_model()
```

Explanation:

- MLflow logs model versions, parameters, and performance metrics.
- Easy rollback if a newer version underperforms.

4. A/B Testing for New Models

Deploy two model versions to compare their performance in production.

Example: A/B Testing Logic

```
import random


def route_request():
```

```
    # Randomly select between Model A and Model B

    model_version = "A" if random.random() < 0.5
else "B"

    return model_version



# Simulate 10 user requests

for _ in range(10):

    print(f"Using Model {route_request()}")
```

Explanation:

- Randomly splits traffic between two model versions.
- Monitor which version performs better.

Best Practices for Continuous Improvement

1. Automate Retraining Pipelines: Reduce manual interventions with automation.
2. Implement CI/CD for Models: Use CI/CD tools (e.g., Jenkins, GitHub Actions) for safe deployments.
3. Use Incremental Learning: Apply online learning for models that need frequent updates.
4. Regularly Monitor Data Drift: Watch for data distribution changes to trigger retraining.
5. Roll Out Gradually: Use canary deployments or A/B testing to minimize risks.
6. Collect and Integrate Feedback: Use user feedback to improve model predictions.
7. Document Everything: Keep detailed records of model versions, data changes, and retraining schedules.

Exercise: Automate Model Improvement

Task:

1. Write a script that monitors model accuracy.
2. If accuracy drops below a threshold, trigger model retraining.
3. Log the updated model version.

Chapter 8: Industry Case Studies and Applications

AI workflows have transformed how industries operate by automating tasks, enhancing decision-making, and creating personalized user experiences. The concepts, tools, and strategies we've explored so far become even more meaningful when applied to real-world scenarios. This chapter presents detailed case studies that demonstrate how organizations across industries are leveraging AI workflows for maximum impact.

8.1 Enterprise Workflow Automation

Enterprise Workflow Automation involves the use of software tools to design, execute, and monitor business processes without manual intervention. This could range from automating simple tasks like data entry to complex processes involving multiple systems and decision-making steps.

Key Components of Workflow Automation

1. Process Mapping: Identify and document workflows to understand how tasks flow across teams.
2. Automation Tools: Implement tools to automate tasks (e.g., task schedulers, AI models, robotic process automation).
3. Integration: Connect different systems, databases, and APIs to ensure seamless data flow.
4. Monitoring and Optimization: Continuously monitor workflows and refine them for better performance.

Benefits of Workflow Automation

- Increased Efficiency: Reduces manual effort and processing time.
- Cost Savings: Cuts down on operational costs by automating labor-intensive tasks.
- Accuracy and Compliance: Minimizes human errors and ensures regulatory compliance.
- Scalability: Easily scales operations without a proportional increase in resources.
- Employee Productivity: Frees employees to focus on creative and strategic tasks.

Real-World Use Case: Automating Employee Onboarding

Problem

A large corporation spends hours manually onboarding new employees, involving repetitive tasks like document collection, account setup, and training assignments.

Solution

An AI-powered workflow was developed to automate the onboarding process, streamlining communication between HR, IT, and the new hires.

Automated Workflow Steps

1. Document Collection: Automated emails to collect and verify necessary documents.
2. Account Creation: API integration with the IT system to create employee accounts.
3. Training Assignments: Automatic enrollment in mandatory training programs.
4. Status Updates: Notifications sent to HR for tracking progress.

Hands-On Example: Automating Employee Onboarding

We'll build a simple Python workflow that automates email notifications and user account creation.

Step 1: Install Required Packages

pip install smtplib schedule pandas

Step 2: Python Script for Workflow Automation

```
import smtplib

from email.mime.text import MIMEText

import pandas as pd

import time

import schedule


# Sample employee data

employees = pd.DataFrame({

    'Name': ['John Doe', 'Jane Smith'],

    'Email': ['john.doe@example.com',
'jane.smith@example.com'],

    'Department': ['IT', 'HR']

})


# Function to send onboarding emails

def send_onboarding_email(name, email):
```

```python
    subject = "Welcome to the Company!"

    body = f"Hi {name},\n\nWelcome aboard! Please
complete your onboarding tasks.\n\nBest,\nHR
Team"

    message = MIMEText(body)

    message['Subject'] = subject

    message['From'] = 'hr@example.com'

    message['To'] = email


    # Simulate sending an email (for
demonstration purposes)

    print(f"Sending email to
{email}...\n{body}\n")


# Function to automate onboarding

def automate_onboarding():

    for _, row in employees.iterrows():

        send_onboarding_email(row['Name'],
row['Email'])

        print(f"Account created for {row['Name']}
in {row['Department']} department.")


# Schedule the task to run every day at 9 AM
```

```
schedule.every().day.at("09:00").do(automate_onbo
arding)


# Run the scheduled task

while True:

    schedule.run_pending()

    time.sleep(60)
```

Explanation

1. Email Notifications: Automatically sends onboarding emails to new employees.
2. Account Creation Simulation: Logs simulated account creation in the relevant department.
3. Scheduling: Automates the process to run daily at 9 AM.

Scaling Workflow Automation

As businesses grow, their workflow automation must scale to handle increased workloads. Scaling involves integrating more advanced tools and ensuring the system can adapt to changing demands.

Strategies for Scaling

1. Integrate with APIs: Connect internal systems (e.g., HR, IT, Finance) for seamless operations.
2. Adopt Robotic Process Automation (RPA): Use bots to handle repetitive, rule-based tasks.
3. Cloud Deployment: Deploy workflows in the cloud for scalability and high availability.
4. Dynamic Resource Allocation: Use autoscaling to handle fluctuating workloads.

Advanced Example: Automating Invoice Processing

In larger enterprises, processing invoices is a resource-intensive task. Let's automate it using OCR for data extraction and validation.

Step 1: Install Required Libraries

```
pip install pytesseract opencv-python pandas
```

Step 2: Python Script for Invoice Processing

```python
import cv2

import pytesseract

import pandas as pd


# Function to extract data from invoice

def extract_invoice_data(image_path):

    image = cv2.imread(image_path)

    text = pytesseract.image_to_string(image)


    # Simple parsing (mock example)

    lines = text.split('\n')

    invoice_number = [line for line in lines if
"Invoice" in line]

    amount = [line for line in lines if "$" in
line]
```

```
    return {"Invoice Number": invoice_number,
"Amount": amount}


# Process a sample invoice

invoice_data =
extract_invoice_data("sample_invoice.jpg")

df = pd.DataFrame([invoice_data])

df.to_csv("processed_invoices.csv", index=False)


print("Invoice data extracted and saved.")
```

Explanation

1. OCR Integration: Extracts text from scanned invoices.
2. Data Parsing: Simplified extraction of invoice numbers and amounts.
3. CSV Export: Saves the extracted data for further processing.

Best Practices for Enterprise Workflow Automation

1. Start Small, Scale Gradually: Begin with automating low-risk, repetitive tasks.
2. Map Processes Thoroughly: Understand the workflow end-to-end before automating.
3. Integrate Systems: Use APIs and cloud services for seamless data flow.
4. Monitor and Optimize: Continuously track performance and improve workflows.

5. Ensure Security and Compliance: Protect sensitive data and comply with regulations.
6. Involve Stakeholders: Engage employees to ensure smooth adoption.

Exercise: Automate a Leave Approval Process

Task:

1. Automate leave request submissions via email.
2. Automatically approve/reject requests based on department workload.
3. Send notifications to employees.

Hint: Use Python with email handling and simple condition checks to simulate approvals.

8.2 AI-Driven Customer Support Solutions

Providing exceptional customer support is essential for any business aiming to build lasting relationships and trust with its customers. However, traditional customer support methods often struggle with handling large volumes of inquiries, inconsistent service quality, and slow response times. AI-driven customer support solutions are transforming this space by offering scalable, efficient, and highly personalized customer service experiences.

Challenges in Traditional Customer Support

1. High Volume of Inquiries: Handling thousands of customer requests can overwhelm human agents.
2. Limited Availability: Human agents typically operate during set hours, leaving customers unsupported after hours.
3. Inconsistent Responses: Human error and varied skill levels can lead to inconsistent service.

4. Costly Operations: Hiring and training support agents is expensive and time-consuming.

How AI Addresses These Challenges

- 24/7 Availability: AI systems can provide support around the clock.
- Instant Responses: AI reduces wait times by instantly responding to common queries.
- Scalability: AI systems can handle thousands of simultaneous interactions.
- Cost Efficiency: Reduces operational costs by automating repetitive tasks.

Key Components of AI-Driven Customer Support

1. Chatbots and Virtual Assistants: AI bots that interact with customers via chat or voice.
2. Natural Language Processing (NLP): Understands and processes human language.
3. Sentiment Analysis: Detects customer emotions to tailor responses.
4. Recommendation Systems: Suggests products or solutions based on customer behavior.
5. Omnichannel Integration: Offers consistent support across chat, email, social media, and phone.

Real-World Example: AI Chatbot for E-commerce

Problem:

A growing e-commerce platform struggled with handling customer inquiries about order status, returns, and product information. The existing support team was overwhelmed, leading to slow responses and dissatisfied customers.

Solution:

An AI-powered chatbot was implemented to automate responses to common queries and escalate complex issues to human agents.

Workflow Breakdown:

1. User Query Handling: The chatbot understands the user's question using NLP.
2. Response Generation: Provides automated responses or gathers more details.
3. Escalation: Complex inquiries are handed off to human agents.

Building a Simple AI Chatbot for Customer Support

Let's create a basic chatbot using **Python** to handle customer inquiries related to order status.

Step 1: Install Required Libraries

```
pip install transformers torch flask
```

Step 2: Python Script for a Customer Support Chatbot

```
from transformers import pipeline

from flask import Flask, request, jsonify


# Initialize the chatbot with a pre-trained
conversational model

chatbot = pipeline("conversational",
model="microsoft/DialoGPT-medium")


# Initialize Flask for API deployment
```

```python
app = Flask(__name__)


@app.route('/chat', methods=['POST'])

def chat():

    user_message = request.json.get("message")

    if not user_message:

        return jsonify({"response": "Please enter
a valid message."}), 400


    # Generate a response

    response =
chatbot(user_message)[0]['generated_text']

    return jsonify({"response": response})


if __name__ == "__main__":

    app.run(port=5000, debug=True)
```

Explanation:

1. NLP Model: We used Microsoft's DialoGPT to generate conversational responses.
2. API Endpoint: The chatbot is deployed as an API using Flask.
3. Response Handling: It generates responses based on the customer's input.

Sample Interaction:

- Customer: "Where is my order?"
- Chatbot: "Please provide your order number to check the status."

Advanced Features for AI Customer Support

1. Intent Recognition: Understanding the intent behind a customer's query is essential for generating relevant responses.

Example: Simple Intent Detection

```python
def detect_intent(message):

    if "order" in message.lower():

        return "order_status"

    elif "refund" in message.lower():

        return "refund_request"

    elif "product" in message.lower():

        return "product_info"

    else:

        return "general_inquiry"


# Test the function

print(detect_intent("I want to check my order status"))   # Output: order_status
```

Explanation:

- Classifies customer queries into different categories for appropriate handling.

2. Escalation to Human Agents: For complex issues, the system should escalate the conversation to a human agent.

Example: Automated Escalation

```
def handle_query(intent):

    if intent == "order_status":

        return "Please provide your order
number."

    elif intent == "refund_request":

        return "I'll connect you to a support
agent for refunds."

    else:

        return "Let me help you with that!"


# Simulated flow

user_input = "I need a refund"

intent = detect_intent(user_input)

print(handle_query(intent))
```

Explanation:

Simple logic determines when to escalate to human agents.

3. Sentiment Analysis: Detecting a customer's emotion allows the system to adapt responses for better service.

Example: Sentiment Detection

```python
from textblob import TextBlob


def detect_sentiment(message):

    sentiment =
TextBlob(message).sentiment.polarity

    if sentiment > 0:

        return "positive"

    elif sentiment < 0:

        return "negative"

    else:

        return "neutral"


# Test the function

print(detect_sentiment("I'm really upset with
this service."))   # Output: negative
```

Explanation:

Negative sentiments can trigger priority handling or escalation.

Best Practices for AI Customer Support Solutions

1. Start Small, Then Scale: Begin with automating common queries and expand to complex issues.
2. Ensure Smooth Escalation: Make it easy for customers to reach human support when needed.
3. Monitor Performance: Track resolution rates, customer satisfaction, and model accuracy.
4. Continuous Learning: Regularly update the chatbot with new data and FAQs.
5. Secure User Data: Comply with data protection laws to safeguard customer data.
6. Provide Omnichannel Support: Integrate across chat, email, phone, and social media for seamless user experiences.

Exercise: Build a Multi-Intent Chatbot

Task:

1. Expand the chatbot to handle multiple intents: order status, refunds, and product information.
2. Integrate sentiment analysis to prioritize negative feedback.
3. Implement a simple escalation system to hand over complex queries to human agents.

8.3 Personalized Learning and Recommendation Systems

In today's information-rich world, users expect tailored experiences that align with their unique needs and preferences. This expectation drives the success of personalized learning systems in education and recommendation systems in entertainment, e-commerce, and content delivery. Personalization not only improves user engagement but also increases satisfaction, retention, and outcomes.

Personalized Learning Systems

Personalized learning systems adapt educational content to fit the learner's pace, interests, and performance. They deliver tailored lessons, resources, and assessments, making learning more engaging and effective.

Recommendation Systems

Recommendation systems suggest products, content, or services based on user preferences and behavior. They are widely used in industries like e-commerce (Amazon), streaming platforms (Netflix, Spotify), and social media (YouTube, TikTok).

Types of Recommendation Systems

1. Content-Based Filtering: Recommends items similar to what the user has liked before, based on item features.

2. Collaborative Filtering: Recommends items based on the preferences of similar users.

3. Hybrid Systems: Combines both content-based and collaborative filtering for better recommendations.

4. Knowledge-Based Systems: Uses explicit information about user needs (e.g., product configuration tools).

Real-World Example: Personalized Learning in an Online Education Platform

Problem:

An online learning platform offers thousands of courses, but many students struggle to find content relevant to their interests and learning goals, resulting in low course completion rates.

Solution:

A personalized recommendation system was implemented to suggest courses based on user behavior, learning pace, and previous course interactions.

Workflow Breakdown:

1. Data Collection: Tracks user behavior (course views, ratings, completion).
2. Profile Building: Builds a user profile based on interests and performance.
3. Recommendation Generation: Suggests courses tailored to the user's profile.
4. Feedback Loop: Continuously improves recommendations based on user feedback.

Building a Simple Recommendation System

Let's create a basic course recommendation system using collaborative filtering with Python.

Step 1: Install Required Libraries

```
pip install pandas scikit-learn
```

Step 2: Python Script for Course Recommendation

```
import pandas as pd

from sklearn.neighbors import NearestNeighbors


# Sample user-course interaction data

data = {

    'User': [1, 1, 2, 2, 3, 3],
```

```python
    'Course': ['Python', 'Data Science',
'Python', 'AI', 'AI', 'Machine Learning'],

    'Rating': [5, 4, 5, 3, 4, 5]

}


# Convert to DataFrame

df = pd.DataFrame(data)


# Pivot data to user-course matrix

user_course_matrix = df.pivot_table(index='User',
columns='Course', values='Rating').fillna(0)


# Collaborative filtering using KNN

model = NearestNeighbors(metric='cosine')

model.fit(user_course_matrix)


# Recommend courses for User 1

user_id = 1

distances, indices =
model.kneighbors([user_course_matrix.loc[user_id]
])
```

```
# Display recommendations

print("Recommended Courses for User 1:")

for idx in indices.flatten():

    if idx != user_id - 1:

        recommended_courses =
user_course_matrix.iloc[idx].nonzero()[0]

        for course in recommended_courses:


print(user_course_matrix.columns[course])
```

Explanation:

1. Data Preparation: A user-course rating matrix is created.
2. Model Training: A K-Nearest Neighbors model finds similar users.
3. Recommendations: Suggests courses based on similar users' interests.

Sample Output:

Recommended Courses for User 1:

AI

Machine Learning

Interpretation:

User 1, who liked Python and Data Science, is now recommending AI and Machine Learning, as similar users rated those courses highly.

Content-Based Filtering Example

Content-based filtering recommends items based on the features of items a user has interacted with.

Step 1: Install Required Libraries

```
pip install scikit-learn
```

Step 2: Python Script for Content-Based Filtering

```python
from sklearn.feature_extraction.text import TfidfVectorizer

from sklearn.metrics.pairwise import linear_kernel


# Sample course descriptions

courses = [

    "Learn Python programming and data analysis",

    "Master data science with Python and R",

    "Introduction to artificial intelligence",

    "Deep learning with TensorFlow and Keras",

    "Machine learning algorithms and models"

]


# Convert course descriptions to TF-IDF features

vectorizer = TfidfVectorizer(stop_words='english')
```

```
tfidf_matrix = vectorizer.fit_transform(courses)


# Compute similarity scores

cosine_sim = linear_kernel(tfidf_matrix,
tfidf_matrix)


# Recommend similar courses

def recommend_course(course_title):

    idx = courses.index(course_title)

    sim_scores = list(enumerate(cosine_sim[idx]))

    sim_scores = sorted(sim_scores, key=lambda x:
x[1], reverse=True)[1:3]


    recommended_courses = [courses[i[0]] for i in
sim_scores]

    return recommended_courses


# Recommend courses similar to Python programming

print("Recommended Courses:")

print(recommend_course("Learn Python programming
and data analysis"))
```

Sample Output:

Recommended Courses:

Master data science with Python and R

Machine learning algorithms and models

Explanation:
This system recommends courses similar in content to the one selected, based on text similarity.

Best Practices for Building Recommendation Systems

1. Data Quality Matters: Use clean, relevant data for better recommendations.
2. Use Hybrid Models: Combine collaborative and content-based filtering for improved accuracy.
3. Monitor and Optimize: Regularly monitor model performance and adjust algorithms.
4. Prioritize Privacy: Handle user data responsibly and comply with data protection regulations.
5. Feedback Loop: Continuously improve recommendations based on user feedback.

Exercise: Create a Hybrid Recommendation System

Task:

1. Combine collaborative filtering and content-based filtering to recommend courses.
2. Use weighted averaging to balance recommendations from both models.
3. Validate performance with user feedback or accuracy metrics.

8.4 Dynamic Data Pipelines in Finance and Healthcare

A dynamic data pipeline is an automated system for collecting, transforming, and delivering data from multiple sources to target systems in real-time or near-real-time. It adapts to changes in data flow, scales with demand, and ensures data integrity.

Key Components of Dynamic Data Pipelines

1. Data Ingestion: Collecting data from various sources (databases, APIs, IoT devices).
2. Data Processing: Cleaning, transforming, and enriching data for analysis.
3. Data Storage: Storing processed data in databases, data warehouses, or data lakes.
4. Data Analysis and Reporting: Real-time analytics, machine learning, or visualization.
5. Monitoring and Error Handling: Detecting and managing failures or data inconsistencies.

Dynamic Data Pipelines in Finance

Use Case: Real-Time Fraud Detection

Problem:
Financial institutions face increasing threats from fraudulent transactions. Traditional systems detect fraud after it occurs, causing financial losses.

Solution:
Implement a real-time data pipeline to monitor transactions and detect fraud instantly using machine learning models.

Pipeline Workflow

1. Data Ingestion: Stream real-time transaction data from payment gateways.
2. Data Processing: Apply data validation and feature engineering.
3. Model Inference: Use a trained model to classify transactions as fraudulent or legitimate.
4. Alerting: Flag suspicious transactions for manual review.

Hands-On Example: Real-Time Fraud Detection Pipeline

Let's build a simplified real-time fraud detection pipeline using Python.

Step 1: Install Required Libraries

```
pip install pandas scikit-learn kafka-python
```

Step 2: Simulating the Data Pipeline

```
import pandas as pd

from sklearn.ensemble import IsolationForest

from kafka import KafkaProducer

import json

import time


# Simulated transaction data

transactions = pd.DataFrame({

    'amount': [100, 200, 50000, 150, 70000, 120],

    'location': ['NY', 'CA', 'TX', 'NY', 'CA',
'TX']
```

```python
})


# Train a simple fraud detection model
model = IsolationForest(contamination=0.1)
model.fit(transactions[['amount']])


# Kafka producer for streaming transactions
producer =
KafkaProducer(bootstrap_servers='localhost:9092',

                            value_serializer=lambda
v: json.dumps(v).encode('utf-8'))


# Stream data to Kafka
for _, row in transactions.iterrows():
    data = row.to_dict()
    prediction =
model.predict([[data['amount']]])
    data['fraud'] = True if prediction[0] == -1
else False
    producer.send('transactions', value=data)
    print(f"Sent: {data}")
    time.sleep(1)
```

Explanation:

- Data Ingestion: Transaction data is streamed using Kafka.
- Model Inference: An Isolation Forest model flags unusual transactions.
- Real-Time Processing: Transactions are streamed in real-time for immediate analysis.

Sample Output:

Sent: {'amount': 50000, 'location': 'TX', 'fraud': True}

Sent: {'amount': 150, 'location': 'NY', 'fraud': False}

Sent: {'amount': 70000, 'location': 'CA', 'fraud': True}

Dynamic Data Pipelines in Healthcare

Use Case: Real-Time Patient Monitoring

Problem:
Hospitals need to monitor patient vitals continuously to detect early signs of health deterioration.

Solution:
Implement a dynamic data pipeline to process real-time data from wearable devices and alert medical staff when abnormal patterns are detected.

Pipeline Workflow

1. Data Ingestion: Collect vitals (heart rate, oxygen levels) from wearable devices.
2. Data Processing: Clean and normalize incoming data streams.

3. Model Inference: Use machine learning models to detect health risks.
4. Alerting: Notify healthcare professionals of anomalies.

Hands-On Example: Patient Health Monitoring Pipeline

Step 1: Install Required Libraries

```
pip install pandas scikit-learn kafka-python
```

Step 2: Simulating Real-Time Health Data Monitoring

```
import pandas as pd

from sklearn.ensemble import
RandomForestClassifier

from kafka import KafkaProducer

import json

import time


# Simulated patient vitals data

patient_data = pd.DataFrame({

    'heart_rate': [75, 80, 120, 70, 150, 78],

    'oxygen_level': [98, 97, 85, 99, 80, 97]

})


# Train a model to detect abnormal vitals
```

```python
labels = [0, 0, 1, 0, 1, 0]  # 1 indicates
abnormal vitals

model = RandomForestClassifier()

model.fit(patient_data, labels)



# Kafka producer for streaming patient vitals

producer =
KafkaProducer(bootstrap_servers='localhost:9092',

                          value_serializer=lambda
v: json.dumps(v).encode('utf-8'))



# Stream data to Kafka

for _, row in patient_data.iterrows():

    data = row.to_dict()

    prediction =
model.predict([list(data.values())])[0]

    data['alert'] = True if prediction == 1 else
False

    producer.send('patient_vitals', value=data)

    print(f"Sent: {data}")

    time.sleep(1)
```

Explanation:

- Data Ingestion: Real-time health data is streamed via Kafka.

- Model Inference: A machine learning model detects health risks.
- Alerting: If abnormal vitals are detected, an alert is triggered.

Sample Output:

Sent: {'heart_rate': 120, 'oxygen_level': 85, 'alert': True}

Sent: {'heart_rate': 75, 'oxygen_level': 98, 'alert': False}

Sent: {'heart_rate': 150, 'oxygen_level': 80, 'alert': True}

Best Practices for Building Dynamic Data Pipelines

1. Ensure Data Security: Encrypt sensitive data, especially in finance and healthcare.
2. Implement Real-Time Monitoring: Track pipeline performance and data integrity.
3. Use Scalable Technologies: Leverage tools like Kafka, Spark, and cloud services.
4. Automate Error Handling: Set up automatic retries and error alerts.
5. Maintain Compliance: Adhere to industry regulations (HIPAA for healthcare, PCI DSS for finance).
6. Optimize for Low Latency: Prioritize low-latency data processing for real-time systems.

Exercise: Build an Anomaly Detection Pipeline

Task:

1. Create a dynamic data pipeline to detect anomalies in server logs.
2. Use machine learning to flag unusual activity.
3. Stream logs in real-time and generate alerts.

8.5 Multi-Agent Systems in Robotics and IoT

A Multi-Agent System (MAS) is a network of autonomous entities (agents) that interact within an environment to achieve individual or collective goals. Each agent operates independently but can communicate and collaborate with other agents to solve complex problems.

Key Characteristics of MAS

1. Autonomy: Agents operate without direct human intervention.
2. Collaboration: Agents share information and coordinate actions.
3. Scalability: Systems can grow by adding more agents.
4. Flexibility: Agents can adapt to dynamic environments.
5. Decentralization: No single point of control; agents manage themselves.

Agents in Robotics and IoT

- Robotics: Robots coordinate to navigate, manipulate objects, and perform tasks.
- IoT: Devices exchange data and automate processes (e.g., smart homes, smart grids).

Real-World Applications of Multi-Agent Systems

1. Robotics: Warehouse Automation

Problem:
Traditional warehouses rely heavily on manual labor, leading to inefficiencies in inventory management and order fulfillment.

Solution:
Autonomous robots equipped with sensors and communication

modules collaborate to manage inventory, transport goods, and fulfill orders.

Workflow:

- Robots divide the warehouse into zones.
- Each robot handles a zone and coordinates with others for smooth logistics.
- Agents communicate to avoid collisions and optimize delivery routes.

2. IoT: Smart Energy Management

Problem:

Managing energy consumption in smart homes and cities is complex due to fluctuating demand and supply.

Solution:

IoT devices act as agents to monitor energy usage, predict consumption, and optimize energy distribution.

Workflow:

- Smart meters monitor real-time energy usage.
- Devices adjust usage based on pricing or demand.
- Communication between devices ensures optimal energy consumption.

Building a Simple Multi-Agent System

Let's build a simplified simulation where robots (agents) collaborate to move items in a warehouse grid. Each robot must avoid collisions and complete delivery tasks efficiently.

Step 1: Install Required Libraries

```
pip install matplotlib numpy
```

Step 2: Python Code for a Multi-Agent Robot System

```python
import numpy as np

import matplotlib.pyplot as plt

import random


# Warehouse grid size

GRID_SIZE = 10


# Number of robots

NUM_ROBOTS = 3


# Initialize warehouse grid

warehouse = np.zeros((GRID_SIZE, GRID_SIZE))


# Robot class

class Robot:

    def __init__(self, robot_id):

        self.id = robot_id

        self.position = [random.randint(0,
GRID_SIZE-1), random.randint(0, GRID_SIZE-1)]
```

```python
        self.target = [random.randint(0,
GRID_SIZE-1), random.randint(0, GRID_SIZE-1)]


    def move(self):
        # Move towards the target
        for i in [0, 1]:
            if self.position[i] < self.target[i]:
                self.position[i] += 1
            elif self.position[i] >
self.target[i]:
                self.position[i] -= 1


    def has_arrived(self):
        return self.position == self.target


# Initialize robots
robots = [Robot(i) for i in range(NUM_ROBOTS)]


# Simulation loop
for step in range(20):
    plt.clf()
```

```python
        plt.title(f"Step {step + 1}")


    for robot in robots:

        if not robot.has_arrived():

            robot.move()

        plt.scatter(robot.position[0],
robot.position[1], label=f'Robot {robot.id}')


    plt.xlim(-1, GRID_SIZE)

    plt.ylim(-1, GRID_SIZE)

    plt.legend()

    plt.pause(0.5)


plt.show()
```

Explanation:

- Agents (Robots): Each robot has a position and a target location.
- Movement: Robots move step-by-step toward their targets.
- Collision Avoidance (Basic): In this example, robots don't collide because their movement is simplified. More complex coordination can be added for real-world applications.
- Visualization: Robots' movements are visualized on a 10x10 grid.

Implementing Communication Between Agents

For agents to work effectively, they need to communicate. Below is an example of how robots can share their positions to avoid collisions.

Collision-Aware Robot Coordination

```
class RobotWithCommunication(Robot):

    def __init__(self, robot_id):

        super().__init__(robot_id)



    def move(self, occupied_positions):
        for i in [0, 1]:

            next_position = self.position.copy()

            if self.position[i] < self.target[i]:

                next_position[i] += 1

            elif self.position[i] >
self.target[i]:

                next_position[i] -= 1



            if tuple(next_position) not in
occupied_positions:

                self.position = next_position



# Initialize communication-aware robots
```

```python
robots = [RobotWithCommunication(i) for i in
range(NUM_ROBOTS)]


# Simulation with communication

for step in range(20):

    plt.clf()

    plt.title(f"Step {step + 1}")


    occupied_positions = {tuple(robot.position)
for robot in robots}


    for robot in robots:

        if not robot.has_arrived():

            robot.move(occupied_positions)

        plt.scatter(robot.position[0],
robot.position[1], label=f'Robot {robot.id}')


    plt.xlim(-1, GRID_SIZE)

    plt.ylim(-1, GRID_SIZE)

    plt.legend()

    plt.pause(0.5)
```

```
plt.show()
```

Explanation:

- Communication: Robots check the positions of others before moving to avoid collisions.
- Coordination: Each robot is aware of other robots' locations, creating a more intelligent navigation system.

Best Practices for Multi-Agent System Design

1. Decentralized Control: Avoid central coordination; enable agents to make decisions independently.
2. Efficient Communication: Use lightweight protocols (e.g., MQTT, ROS) for agent communication.
3. Fault Tolerance: Design systems that can handle agent failure without compromising the whole system.
4. Dynamic Adaptation: Agents should adapt to environmental changes in real-time.
5. Scalability: Design systems that can scale by adding more agents without significant performance degradation.

Exercise: Expand the Robot System

Task:

1. Implement obstacle avoidance by adding random obstacles to the grid.
2. Introduce task sharing—if one robot is overloaded, another robot should help.
3. Add energy consumption tracking for each robot to simulate battery usage.

Chapter 9: Hands-On Projects and Tutorials

Learning theoretical concepts is essential, but putting those concepts into practice is where the real learning happens. This chapter is dedicated to hands-on projects and tutorials that allow you to apply what you've learned throughout this book. These projects will give you practical experience building real-world AI workflows and systems using LangChain, LangGraph, and related tools.

9.1 Project 1: Building a Context-Aware Chatbot

Chatbots have become a cornerstone of modern user interaction, providing instant responses and automating customer service tasks. However, most basic chatbots fail to offer engaging and human-like conversations because they lack context awareness. A context-aware chatbot remembers previous interactions and adapts responses based on the ongoing conversation. This makes interactions feel more natural and personalized.

In this project, we will build a context-aware chatbot using Python, LangChain, and OpenAI's GPT models. This chatbot will maintain conversation history and deliver relevant, consistent replies throughout the interaction.

Project Overview

Objective

Develop a chatbot that can:

- Understand and remember the context of conversations.
- Handle user queries intelligently and naturally.
- Escalate complex queries to human support when necessary.

Tools and Technologies

- Python 3.8+
- LangChain (for workflow management)
- OpenAI GPT-3/4 (for conversational intelligence)
- Flask (for deploying the chatbot as an API)

Step-by-Step Implementation

Step 1: Setting Up the Environment

Start by installing the required libraries.

```
pip install langchain openai flask python-dotenv
```

Note:
 You need an OpenAI API key. Create a .env file in your project directory and add your API key:

```
OPENAI_API_KEY=your_openai_api_key
```

Step 2: Building the Chatbot with Context Awareness

```
import os

from flask import Flask, request, jsonify

from langchain import OpenAI

from langchain.memory import
ConversationBufferMemory

from langchain.chains import ConversationChain
```

```python
from dotenv import load_dotenv


# Load environment variables

load_dotenv()

openai_api_key = os.getenv("OPENAI_API_KEY")


# Initialize Flask app

app = Flask(__name__)


# Set up OpenAI language model

llm = OpenAI(temperature=0.7,
openai_api_key=openai_api_key)


# Add conversation memory to retain context

memory = ConversationBufferMemory()


# Create a conversation chain

chatbot = ConversationChain(llm=llm,
memory=memory)


@app.route('/chat', methods=['POST'])
```

```python
def chat():

    user_message = request.json.get('message')

    if not user_message:

        return jsonify({'response': "Please enter
a valid message."}), 400



    # Generate response while maintaining
conversation context

    response = chatbot.run(user_message)

    return jsonify({'response': response})



if __name__ == "__main__":

    app.run(port=5000, debug=True)
```

Explanation of the Code

- Flask sets up a lightweight web server to handle chat interactions.
- LangChain's ConversationBufferMemory retains the conversation history.
- OpenAI GPT is used to generate contextually relevant responses.
- The /chat endpoint allows clients to send user messages and receive responses.

Step 3: Testing the Chatbot

You can interact with the chatbot using a tool like Postman or curl.

Example Request:

```
curl -X POST http://127.0.0.1:5000/chat \

-H "Content-Type: application/json" \

-d '{"message": "Hi, how are you?"}'
```

Expected Response:

```
{

  "response": "I'm doing well, thank you! How can
I assist you today?"

}
```

Context-Awareness Test:

1. User: "I need help with my order."
2. Bot: "Sure! Can you provide your order number?"
3. User: "It's 12345."
4. Bot: "Thank you! Let me check the details for order #12345."

The bot remembers that the user is asking about an order and continues the conversation naturally.

Step 4: Enhancing the Chatbot with Intent Recognition

A context-aware chatbot is more effective when it understands the intent behind the user's message. Let's add simple intent detection.

```
def detect_intent(message):

    message = message.lower()

    if "order" in message:
```

```python
        return "order_status"

    elif "refund" in message:

        return "refund_request"

    elif "hello" in message or "hi" in message:

        return "greeting"

    else:

        return "general"


@app.route('/chat', methods=['POST'])

def chat():

    user_message = request.json.get('message')

    if not user_message:

        return jsonify({'response': "Please enter
a valid message."}), 400


    intent = detect_intent(user_message)


    if intent == "order_status":

        response = "Please provide your order
number."

    elif intent == "refund_request":
```

```
    response = "I can help with your refund.
Could you share your order number?"

    elif intent == "greeting":

        response = "Hello! How can I assist you
today?"

    else:

        response = chatbot.run(user_message)



    return jsonify({'response': response})
```

Explanation

- Intent Detection categorizes user input and tailors responses accordingly.
- Fallback to Chatbot: If the intent is unclear, the chatbot continues the conversation naturally.

Step 5: Adding Escalation to Human Agents

For complex queries, it's practical to escalate the conversation to human support.

```
def check_escalation(message):

    keywords = ["speak to someone", "human
agent", "customer service"]

    return any(keyword in message.lower() for
keyword in keywords)



@app.route('/chat', methods=['POST'])
```

```python
def chat():

    user_message = request.json.get('message')

    if not user_message:

        return jsonify({'response': "Please enter
a valid message."}), 400


    if check_escalation(user_message):

        return jsonify({'response': "I am
transferring you to a human agent. Please hold
on."})


    response = chatbot.run(user_message)

    return jsonify({'response': response})
```

Explanation

- If the user requests to speak to a human, the chatbot escalates the conversation.
- Otherwise, it continues responding as usual.

Project Challenges and Considerations

1. Handling Ambiguity: Users may send unclear queries. Implement clarifying questions to refine understanding.

2. Memory Management: Long conversations may overload memory. Use session-based memory to manage context effectively.

3. Data Privacy: Store and process user data securely, especially when handling sensitive information.

4. Scalability: Deploy the chatbot on scalable cloud services to handle more users efficiently.

Exercise: Enhance the Chatbot

Tasks:

1. Implement user authentication to personalize responses.
2. Add logging for conversations to analyze user behavior.
3. Integrate third-party APIs (e.g., weather, news) for dynamic information.

9.2 Project 2: Automating a Data Analysis Pipeline

Data analysis is a cornerstone of decision-making across industries. However, manually processing, cleaning, analyzing, and reporting data can be tedious, error-prone, and inefficient. Automating this process ensures consistency, saves time, and allows businesses to make data-driven decisions faster.

In this project, we will build an automated data analysis pipeline. This pipeline will load raw data, clean it, perform analysis, and generate visual reports—all without manual intervention. This solution can easily scale for larger datasets and more complex workflows.

Project Overview

Objective

Develop a fully automated data analysis pipeline that:

1. Ingests Data: Loads data from a CSV file or database.
2. Cleans Data: Handles missing values, duplicates, and incorrect data types.
3. Analyzes Data: Performs statistical analysis and feature engineering.
4. Visualizes Results: Generates meaningful visual reports.
5. Automates Execution: Runs on a schedule or in response to new data.

Tools and Technologies

- Python 3.8+
- Pandas (Data manipulation)
- Matplotlib/Seaborn (Data visualization)
- LangChain (Workflow automation)
- Schedule (Task automation)

Step-by-Step Implementation

Step 1: Install Required Libraries

```
pip install pandas matplotlib seaborn langchain
schedule
```

Step 2: Setting Up the Pipeline Structure

Let's break the pipeline into four modular stages:

1. Data Ingestion
2. Data Cleaning
3. Data Analysis
4. Data Visualization

Step 3: Building the Pipeline

1. Data Ingestion

This component loads the raw data from a CSV file.

```
import pandas as pd


def load_data(file_path):

    try:

        data = pd.read_csv(file_path)

        print("Data loaded successfully.")

        return data

    except Exception as e:

        print(f"Error loading data: {e}")

        return None
```

Explanation:

- Reads a CSV file and returns a DataFrame.
- Handles errors gracefully.

2. Data Cleaning

This component cleans the data by handling missing values and duplicates.

```
def clean_data(data):

    # Drop duplicate rows

    data = data.drop_duplicates()


    # Fill missing numerical values with the
median
```

```
    for col in
data.select_dtypes(include='number').columns:

        data[col].fillna(data[col].median(),
inplace=True)



    # Fill missing categorical values with the
mode

    for col in
data.select_dtypes(include='object').columns:

        data[col].fillna(data[col].mode()[0],
inplace=True)



    print("Data cleaned successfully.")

    return data
```

Explanation:

- Duplicates are removed to avoid redundancy.
- Missing values in numerical columns are filled with the median.
- Categorical values are filled with the mode.

3. Data Analysis

This component performs statistical analysis to uncover insights.

```
def analyze_data(data):

    print("\nBasic Statistics:\n",
data.describe())
```

```
# Correlation analysis

correlation_matrix = data.corr()

print("\nCorrelation Matrix:\n",
correlation_matrix)



return correlation_matrix
```

Explanation:

- Descriptive statistics provide an overview of data distribution.
- Correlation analysis identifies relationships between variables.

---

4. Data Visualization

This component generates visual insights.

```
import matplotlib.pyplot as plt

import seaborn as sns


def visualize_data(data, correlation_matrix):

    plt.figure(figsize=(10, 6))
```

```
# Plot correlation heatmap

sns.heatmap(correlation_matrix, annot=True,
cmap='coolwarm', linewidths=0.5)

plt.title('Correlation Heatmap')

plt.savefig('correlation_heatmap.png')

plt.close()


# Plot histogram for numerical data

data.hist(figsize=(10, 8))

plt.tight_layout()

plt.savefig('data_distribution.png')


print("Visual reports generated and saved.")
```

Explanation:

- A heatmap shows correlations between numerical features.
- Histograms reveal the distribution of each numerical feature.

Step 4: Automating the Workflow with LangChain

We will now tie these components together into a seamless pipeline.

```
from langchain.chains import SimpleChain
```

```
# Define the pipeline steps

pipeline = SimpleChain(steps=[

    load_data,

    clean_data,

    analyze_data,

    visualize_data

])
```

```
# Run the pipeline

pipeline.run("sales_data.csv")
```

Explanation:

- LangChain's SimpleChain executes the workflow sequentially.
- All steps are automated, from loading data to generating reports.

Step 5: Scheduling the Pipeline

To automate the pipeline regularly, we can schedule it to run daily.

```
import schedule

import time


def run_pipeline():

    pipeline.run("sales_data.csv")
```

```
# Schedule the pipeline to run every day at 8 AM

schedule.every().day.at("08:00").do(run_pipeline)


print("Pipeline scheduled. Waiting for
execution...")


while True:

    schedule.run_pending()

    time.sleep(60)
```

Explanation:

- The pipeline will automatically run at 8 AM every day.
- Schedule handles task automation without manual triggering.

Sample Output

Once the pipeline runs, you will see:

Console Output:

Data loaded successfully.

Data cleaned successfully.

Basic Statistics:

Sales   Profit

`count`   `100.000000`   `100.000000`

```
mean      500.000000      50.000000
```

. . .

```
Visual reports generated and saved.
```

Generated Files:

- correlation_heatmap.png
- data_distribution.png

These reports provide a visual and statistical summary of the data.

Best Practices for Data Pipeline Automation

1. Error Handling: Implement logging and exception handling for each step.
2. Modularity: Keep each component (ingestion, cleaning, analysis) independent for scalability.
3. Scalability: Use distributed tools (like Apache Airflow) for larger datasets.
4. Monitoring: Set up notifications for pipeline failures or critical errors.
5. Security: Secure data storage and transfer, especially with sensitive data.

Exercise: Enhance the Pipeline

1. Data Source Expansion: Extend the pipeline to load data from APIs or databases.
2. Advanced Analytics: Integrate machine learning models for predictive analysis.
3. Real-Time Processing: Implement real-time data processing using Kafka or Spark.
4. Email Reports: Automate email notifications with attached reports after each run.

9.3 Project 3: Designing a Multi-Agent Task Manager

In this project, you'll design a **Multi-Agent Task Manager** where agents collaborate to execute and manage tasks effectively. This setup can be applied in various industries—from logistics and operations to robotics and cloud computing—where multiple tasks need to be processed concurrently.

This project will guide you step-by-step to build a working Multi-Agent Task Manager using Python with realistic features like dynamic task allocation, load balancing, and fault tolerance.

Project Overview

Objective

- Develop a system where multiple agents can autonomously manage and execute tasks.
- Implement dynamic task allocation, load balancing, and error handling.
- Design a scalable and fault-tolerant task management workflow.

Tools and Technologies

- `Python 3.8+`
- `Threading for concurrent task execution`
- `Queue for task distribution`
- `Logging for real-time monitoring`

```
System Design
```

```
Key Components
```

1. Task Manager: Central coordinator that distributes tasks among agents.
2. Worker Agents: Independent agents that pick up and execute tasks.
3. Task Queue: Organizes and holds tasks before assignment.
4. Monitoring and Fault Tolerance: Tracks task progress and handles failures.

Workflow

1. Tasks are added to a shared Task Queue.
2. Worker Agents continuously request and execute tasks.
3. The Task Manager monitors progress and reallocates tasks if necessary.

Step-by-Step Implementation

Step 1: Install Required Libraries

No additional libraries are required beyond Python's standard library.

```
pip install tqdm
```

Step 2: Define the Task Manager

The Task Manager will distribute tasks and monitor progress.

```
from queue import Queue
```

```python
class TaskManager:

    def __init__(self, tasks):
        self.task_queue = Queue()
        self.completed_tasks = []

        for task in tasks:
            self.task_queue.put(task)

    def assign_task(self):
        if not self.task_queue.empty():
            return self.task_queue.get()
        return None

    def mark_task_complete(self, task):
        self.completed_tasks.append(task)

    def is_all_done(self):
        return self.task_queue.empty()
```

Explanation:

- Initializes a queue with all tasks.
- Provides methods to assign tasks and mark them as completed.
- Tracks task completion status.

Step 3: Create Worker Agents

Worker Agents will independently execute assigned tasks.

```python
import threading

import time

import random


class WorkerAgent(threading.Thread):

    def __init__(self, agent_id, task_manager):

        super().__init__()

        self.agent_id = agent_id

        self.task_manager = task_manager


    def run(self):

        while not self.task_manager.is_all_done():
```

```
            task =
self.task_manager.assign_task()

        if task:

            print(f"Agent {self.agent_id} is
working on {task}")

            self.execute_task(task)


self.task_manager.mark_task_complete(task)

            print(f"Agent {self.agent_id}
completed {task}")

        else:

            time.sleep(1)   # Wait if no task
is available


    def execute_task(self, task):

        # Simulate task execution time

        execution_time = random.randint(1, 3)

        time.sleep(execution_time)
```

Explanation:

- Each agent runs in its own thread for concurrent execution.
- Agents continuously check for available tasks and execute them.
- Task execution time is randomized to simulate real-world conditions.

Step 4: Putting It All Together

Now, let's combine the Task Manager and Worker Agents.

```python
if __name__ == "__main__":

    # Define tasks

    tasks = [f"Task-{i}" for i in range(1, 11)]
    # 10 tasks


    # Initialize Task Manager

    task_manager = TaskManager(tasks)


    # Create 3 worker agents

    agents = [WorkerAgent(agent_id=i,
    task_manager=task_manager) for i in range(3)]


    # Start all agents

    for agent in agents:

        agent.start()


    # Wait for all agents to complete

    for agent in agents:

        agent.join()
```

```
print("All tasks have been completed.")
```

Expected Output:

Agent 0 is working on Task-1

Agent 1 is working on Task-2

Agent 2 is working on Task-3

Agent 0 completed Task-1

Agent 0 is working on Task-4

...

All tasks have been completed.

Step 5: Adding Fault Tolerance

Let's simulate real-world conditions where tasks might fail and need to be retried.

```
class WorkerAgentWithRetry(threading.Thread):

    def __init__(self, agent_id, task_manager,
max_retries=2):

        super().__init__()

        self.agent_id = agent_id

        self.task_manager = task_manager

        self.max_retries = max_retries
```

```python
    def run(self):

        while not
self.task_manager.is_all_done():

            task =
self.task_manager.assign_task()

            if task:

                success = self.execute_task(task)

                if not success:

                    print(f"Agent {self.agent_id}
failed {task}, retrying...")

self.task_manager.task_queue.put(task)

                else:

self.task_manager.mark_task_complete(task)

                    print(f"Agent {self.agent_id}
completed {task}")

            else:

                time.sleep(1)


    def execute_task(self, task):

        execution_time = random.randint(1, 3)

        time.sleep(execution_time)
```

```
# Simulate a random failure

return random.choice([True, False])
```

Explanation:

- 20-50% chance that a task will fail.
- Failed tasks are requeued for another agent to retry.
- Agents handle failures gracefully.

Step 6: Real-Time Monitoring

Let's monitor the task progress in real-time.

```
from tqdm import tqdm


class TaskManagerWithProgress(TaskManager):

    def __init__(self, tasks):

        super().__init__(tasks)

        self.progress_bar =
tqdm(total=len(tasks), desc="Task Progress")


    def mark_task_complete(self, task):

        super().mark_task_complete(task)

        self.progress_bar.update(1)
```

Explanation:

- A progress bar visually tracks task completion.

- Enhances user experience by showing real-time updates.

Best Practices for Multi-Agent Systems

1. Load Balancing: Distribute tasks fairly to prevent bottlenecks.
2. Fault Tolerance: Implement retries for failed tasks.
3. Scalability: Design the system to easily add more agents.
4. Resource Management: Prevent agents from overusing system resources.
5. Monitoring: Track progress and performance with real-time report

Exercise: Enhance the Task Manager

1. Priority Queues: Implement task prioritization (urgent tasks first).
2. Specialized Agents: Assign certain agents to specific types of tasks.
3. Dynamic Scaling: Automatically adjust the number of agents based on workload.
4. Logging: Add logging for detailed audit trails of agent performance.

9.4 Best Practices for Scalable AI Projects

Scaling AI projects from prototypes to production-ready systems presents numerous challenges. An AI system that works well in development can falter when deployed at scale due to issues like data bottlenecks, inefficient resource management, or integration failures. Building scalable AI solutions requires thoughtful design, robust infrastructure, and proactive maintenance.

1. Design for Scalability from the Start

Many AI projects fail to scale because scalability wasn't considered during the design phase. Building scalability into the architecture upfront prevents costly redesigns later.

Best Practices

- Modular Architecture: Break the system into independent modules (data processing, model training, inference, monitoring) to allow individual scaling.
- Microservices: Use microservices to decouple components and scale them independently.
- Stateless Services: Design services to be stateless where possible, making them easier to distribute across servers.

Example

```
# Example of a modular ML pipeline

def data_preprocessing(data):

    # Clean and prepare data

    pass


def model_training(processed_data):

    # Train the model

    pass


def model_inference(model, input_data):

    # Make predictions

    pass
```

Each function is modular and can be scaled or updated independently.

2. Automate Everything

Manual workflows don't scale well. Automating your workflows reduces errors and saves time, especially when deploying models or handling large datasets.

Best Practices

- CI/CD Pipelines: Automate testing, deployment, and scaling.
- Automated Data Pipelines: Use tools like Apache Airflow or Prefect for data pipeline automation.
- Model Retraining: Automate model retraining with fresh data using triggers or scheduled jobs.

Example: Automating Model Deployment with CI/CD

```
# Example GitHub Actions workflow for ML
deployment

name: Deploy Model


on:

  push:

    branches:

      - main


jobs:
```

```
deploy:

  runs-on: ubuntu-latest


  steps:

    - name: Checkout Repository

      uses: actions/checkout@v2


    - name: Install Dependencies

      run: pip install -r requirements.txt


    - name: Run Tests

      run: pytest tests/


    - name: Deploy Model

      run: python deploy.py
```

Every time you push changes, the model is automatically tested and deployed.

3. Optimize Data Handling

Efficient data handling is crucial for scalable AI systems. Slow data pipelines or memory issues can cripple performance as data volume grows.

Best Practices

- Batch Processing: Process data in batches instead of loading entire datasets into memory.
- Data Sharding: Split large datasets into smaller, manageable chunks.
- Use Efficient Formats: Store data in efficient formats like Parquet or Avro for big data processing.

Example: Batch Data Processing

```python
import pandas as pd


def process_in_batches(file_path, batch_size):

    for chunk in pd.read_csv(file_path,
chunksize=batch_size):

        # Process each batch

        print(chunk.head())


process_in_batches("large_dataset.csv",
batch_size=10000)
```

Loading data in chunks prevents memory overflow and allows parallel processing.

4. Use Distributed Computing

When datasets or models grow, a single machine may not be sufficient. Distributed computing helps you process data and train models across multiple machines.

Best Practices

- Parallel Processing: Use Python's multiprocessing or tools like Dask for parallel execution.
- Cloud Services: Leverage cloud platforms (AWS, GCP, Azure) for distributed training and deployment.
- Data Partitioning: Split data across nodes to balance workloads.

Example: Parallel Data Processing with Dask

```python
import dask.dataframe as dd


# Load large CSV with Dask

df = dd.read_csv('large_dataset.csv')


# Perform parallel operations

result = df.groupby('category').mean().compute()

print(result)
```

Dask automatically splits data processing across multiple CPU cores or machines.

5. Optimize Model Performance

Models that work well on small datasets may not perform efficiently on large datasets or in production. Optimization ensures the model scales with the demand.

Best Practices

- Model Compression: Use quantization or pruning to reduce model size.

- Efficient Models: Choose models that balance accuracy and inference speed.
- Hardware Acceleration: Use GPUs or TPUs for training and inference.

Example: Using Quantization for Model Compression

```
import tensorflow as tf


# Load model

model = tf.keras.models.load_model('model.h5')


# Convert to TensorFlow Lite with quantization

converter =
tf.lite.TFLiteConverter.from_keras_model(model)

converter.optimizations =
[tf.lite.Optimize.DEFAULT]

tflite_model = converter.convert()


# Save the quantized model

with open('model_quantized.tflite', 'wb') as f:

    f.write(tflite_model)
```

Quantization reduces model size and speeds up inference without significant accuracy loss.

6. Implement Robust Monitoring and Logging

Without monitoring, it's hard to know how your system is performing or why it might be failing. Monitoring ensures that your system remains scalable, reliable, and efficient.

Best Practices

- Model Drift Detection: Monitor changes in input data and model predictions.
- Resource Monitoring: Track CPU, memory, and GPU usage.
- Error Logging: Implement detailed logging for debugging and audits.

Example: Monitoring with Prometheus

```
# prometheus.yml configuration

global:

  scrape_interval: 15s


scrape_configs:

  - job_name: 'model_monitor'

    static_configs:

      - targets: ['localhost:8000']
```

Regular monitoring detects performance degradation early, allowing for timely intervention.

7. Design for Failures

Failures in distributed systems are inevitable. Building resilience ensures that the system can recover from failures without data loss or downtime.

Best Practices

- Graceful Failures: Implement fallback mechanisms when a component fails.
- Redundancy: Use redundant resources to prevent single points of failure.
- Retries and Timeouts: Handle failures with retries and exponential backoff.

Example: Retry with Exponential Backoff

```python
import time

import random


def fetch_data():

    if random.random() < 0.7:

        raise Exception("Temporary failure")

    return "Data fetched"


def retry_fetch(retries=3):

    for i in range(retries):

        try:

            return fetch_data()

        except Exception as e:

            wait = 2 ** i
```

```
        print(f"Retrying in {wait}
seconds...")

        time.sleep(wait)

    raise Exception("Failed after retries")



print(retry_fetch())
```

Exponential backoff reduces system overload and increases recovery chances after failure.

8. Secure Your AI System

Security is critical when handling sensitive data and deploying models in production.

Best Practices

- Data Encryption: Encrypt data in transit and at rest.
- Access Control: Implement role-based access control (RBAC).
- Regular Audits: Conduct regular security audits.

Adopting these practices will ensure that your AI projects remain maintainable and effective as they grow, empowering you to deliver impactful solutions in real-world environments.

9.5 Common Pitfalls and Troubleshooting

Developing scalable AI projects is a complex and iterative process. Even the most well-designed systems can run into problems if critical details are overlooked. Understanding the most common pitfalls and knowing how to troubleshoot them is essential for building robust, reliable AI systems. This section will discuss some of the most frequent challenges in AI project development and deployment, with practical solutions and code examples to help you avoid or resolve them.

1. Poor Data Quality

The Problem

Garbage in, garbage out. If your input data is inaccurate, incomplete, or biased, your model's performance will suffer regardless of how sophisticated it is.

Common Symptoms

- Inconsistent predictions
- Poor model accuracy
- Overfitting to noisy or irrelevant data

How to Fix It

- Data Validation: Implement checks to detect missing or corrupt data.
- Data Cleaning: Handle missing values, remove duplicates, and correct inconsistent entries.
- Bias Detection: Analyze data distributions to ensure balanced representation.

Code Example: Data Validation

```
import pandas as pd


def validate_data(file_path):

    data = pd.read_csv(file_path)
```

```python
    # Check for missing values
    if data.isnull().values.any():
        print("Warning: Missing values
detected!")


    # Check for duplicates
    if data.duplicated().any():
        print("Warning: Duplicate records
detected!")


    # Check data types
    print("Data types:\n", data.dtypes)


validate_data("dataset.csv")
```

Solution Explanation:
This script flags missing values, duplicate records, and data type mismatches, ensuring the data is clean before training the model.

2. Overfitting and Underfitting

The Problem

- Overfitting: The model performs well on training data but poorly on unseen data.
- Underfitting: The model is too simple and fails to capture underlying data patterns.

Common Symptoms

- High accuracy on training data but low accuracy on test data.
- Very low accuracy across all datasets.

How to Fix It

- Overfitting: Use regularization, dropout layers, and reduce model complexity.
- Underfitting: Use more complex models, increase training time, or provide more relevant features.

Code Example: Applying Regularization

```python
from sklearn.linear_model import Ridge

from sklearn.model_selection import train_test_split

from sklearn.metrics import mean_squared_error

import pandas as pd


# Load dataset

data = pd.read_csv("dataset.csv")

X = data.drop("target", axis=1)

y = data["target"]


# Split data
```

```
X_train, X_test, y_train, y_test =
train_test_split(X, y, test_size=0.2)


# Ridge Regression to prevent overfitting

model = Ridge(alpha=1.0)

model.fit(X_train, y_train)


# Evaluate

predictions = model.predict(X_test)

print("MSE:", mean_squared_error(y_test,
predictions))
```

Solution Explanation:
The Ridge regression model applies **L2 regularization** to penalize large coefficients and reduce overfitting.

3. Data Leakage

The Problem

Data leakage occurs when information from outside the training dataset leaks into the model during training, leading to unrealistically high performance.

Common Symptoms

- Extremely high accuracy during training but poor performance in production.
- Fast convergence without generalizing well.

How to Fix It

- Strict Data Separation: Always separate training, validation, and test datasets.
- Pipeline Integration: Ensure preprocessing is applied only to training data during fitting.

Code Example: Proper Data Splitting

```python
from sklearn.preprocessing import StandardScaler

from sklearn.pipeline import Pipeline

from sklearn.linear_model import
LogisticRegression

from sklearn.model_selection import
train_test_split


# Split data first

X_train, X_test, y_train, y_test =
train_test_split(X, y, test_size=0.2)


# Apply scaling only on training data

pipeline = Pipeline([

    ('scaler', StandardScaler()),

    ('classifier', LogisticRegression())

])


pipeline.fit(X_train, y_train)
```

```
accuracy = pipeline.score(X_test, y_test)

print("Model accuracy:", accuracy)
```

Solution Explanation:

The pipeline ensures that **StandardScaler** is only fitted on the training set, preventing data leakage into the test set.

4. Inefficient Model Deployment

The Problem

Many AI models work well in development but fail in production due to inefficient deployment practices.

Common Symptoms

- Long response times during inference
- High memory or CPU usage in production
- Crashes under high load

How to Fix It

- Model Compression: Use quantization or pruning to reduce model size.
- Batch Inference: Process predictions in batches for efficiency.
- Containerization: Deploy using Docker or Kubernetes for scalability.

Code Example: Batch Prediction

```
import numpy as np

from sklearn.linear_model import
LogisticRegression
```

```
# Simulate a trained model

model = LogisticRegression()

model.fit(X_train, y_train)


# Batch inference function

def batch_predict(model, data, batch_size=100):

    predictions = []

    for i in range(0, len(data), batch_size):

        batch = data[i:i+batch_size]

        predictions.extend(model.predict(batch))

    return predictions


batch_predictions = batch_predict(model, X_test)

print(batch_predictions)
```

Solution Explanation:
Batch prediction improves performance by reducing the overhead of making single predictions repeatedly.

5. Lack of Monitoring and Logging

The Problem

Without proper monitoring, it's impossible to detect failures, performance degradation, or data drift in production models.

Common Symptoms

- Unexpected prediction errors in production
- No insight into system performance
- Difficulty debugging issues

How to Fix It

- Performance Monitoring: Track inference times, error rates, and resource utilization.
- Model Drift Detection: Monitor input data distributions and output changes.
- Comprehensive Logging: Implement detailed logs for system behavior.

Code Example: Basic Model Monitoring

```python
import logging

import time



# Configure logging

logging.basicConfig(filename='model.log',
level=logging.INFO)



def predict_with_monitoring(model, data):

    start_time = time.time()

    predictions = model.predict(data)

    end_time = time.time()
```

```
logging.info(f"Prediction completed in
{end_time - start_time} seconds")

return predictions
```

```
predict_with_monitoring(model, X_test)
```

Solution Explanation:
This logs the model's prediction time, which can help monitor performance over time.

6. Ignoring Scalability Concerns

The Problem

AI systems designed without scalability in mind often struggle when data volume or user demand grows.

Common Symptoms

- Slow model response times with increased traffic
- Crashes during high load
- Inability to handle large datasets

How to Fix It

- Asynchronous Processing: Use async operations to handle large workloads.
- Cloud Deployment: Scale using cloud services (AWS, GCP, Azure).
- Distributed Systems: Use Spark or Dask for large data processing.

Code Example: Asynchronous API with FastAPI

```
from fastapi import FastAPI
```

```
import asyncio


app = FastAPI()


@app.get("/predict")

async def predict():

    await asyncio.sleep(2)   # Simulate processing
delay

    return {"result": "Prediction completed"}
```

Solution Explanation:
Using async allows the API to handle more requests concurrently, improving scalability.

By anticipating these challenges and applying the troubleshooting strategies shared here, you can build AI systems that perform reliably and scale effectively in production environments.

Chapter 10: Future Trends and Innovations in AI Workflows

In this chapter, we'll explore upcoming trends and innovations in AI workflows, focusing on how LangChain and LangGraph are poised to adapt and integrate with emerging technologies. We'll also discuss the growing role of open-source communities and share predictions about the future of dynamic AI systems.

10.1 Evolving AI Agent Architectures

AI agents have come a long way from their early, rule-based designs. Modern AI systems demand more than simple input-output interactions—they require adaptability, autonomy, and the ability to handle complex, dynamic environments. This evolution in AI agent architectures is driven by the need for intelligent systems that can think, learn, and collaborate more effectively.

An AI agent is a system capable of perceiving its environment, processing information, and taking actions to achieve specific goals. Over the years, agent architectures have evolved into more complex and capable models, addressing limitations of earlier designs.

Key Characteristics of Modern AI Agents

1. Autonomy: Agents operate independently, making decisions without constant human input.
2. Reactivity: Agents respond to changes in their environment in real-time.
3. Proactivity: Agents initiate actions to achieve goals, rather than only reacting.

4. Social Ability: Agents can collaborate and communicate with other agents or systems.

Evolution of AI Agent Architectures

1. Reactive Agents

Reactive agents are designed to respond directly to environmental stimuli. They follow a set of predefined rules and react without any internal representation of the world.

Example:
A simple thermostat that turns on the heater when the temperature drops below a set point.

Limitation:
Reactive agents lack memory and cannot plan or learn from past experiences.

2. Deliberative Agents

Deliberative agents build an internal model of the environment and make decisions by reasoning over this model. They can plan actions in advance and adjust their behavior based on goals.

Example:
A chess-playing AI that plans several moves ahead based on the opponent's possible moves.

Limitation:
These agents can be slow in dynamic environments because reasoning takes time.

3. Hybrid Agents

Hybrid agents combine reactive and deliberative components, balancing immediate responses with long-term planning.

Example:
A self-driving car that reacts quickly to sudden obstacles (reactive) while following a planned route to its destination (deliberative).

4. Cognitive and Adaptive Agents

Cognitive agents are more sophisticated, capable of learning, adapting, and improving over time. They can use machine learning techniques to adjust their strategies based on experience.

Example:
Recommendation systems like Netflix, which adapt to user preferences over time.

Modern Multi-Layered AI Agent Architectures

A modern AI agent architecture typically includes the following layers:

1. Perception Layer: Gathers data from sensors or inputs.
2. Processing Layer: Analyzes data, performs reasoning, and makes decisions.
3. Action Layer: Executes actions in the environment.
4. Learning Layer: Continuously improves by learning from feedback and data.
5. Communication Layer: Enables interaction with other agents or systems.

Hands-On Example: Building a Hybrid AI Agent

Let's build a simple Hybrid Agent in Python that combines both reactive and deliberative behaviors. The agent will navigate a grid world to reach a target while avoiding obstacles.

Step 1: Install Required Library

```
pip install numpy
```

Step 2: Define the Environment

```python
import numpy as np


class GridWorld:
    def __init__(self, size, obstacles, goal):
        self.size = size
        self.obstacles = obstacles
        self.goal = goal
        self.agent_pos = [0, 0]

    def is_goal_reached(self):
        return self.agent_pos == self.goal

    def is_obstacle(self, pos):
        return pos in self.obstacles

    def move_agent(self, direction):
        moves = {
            "up": [-1, 0],
            "down": [1, 0],
```

```python
        "left": [0, -1],

        "right": [0, 1]

    }

    new_pos = [self.agent_pos[0] +
moves[direction][0],

            self.agent_pos[1] +
moves[direction][1]]


    if (0 <= new_pos[0] < self.size and

        0 <= new_pos[1] < self.size and

        not self.is_obstacle(new_pos)):

        self.agent_pos = new_pos

        return True

    return False
```

Explanation:

A grid world where the agent must navigate to a goal while avoiding obstacles.

Step 3: Create the Hybrid Agent

```python
import random


class HybridAgent:

    def __init__(self, environment):
```

```python
        self.env = environment


    def reactive_behavior(self):
        # Quickly avoid obstacles
        directions = ["up", "down", "left",
"right"]
        random.shuffle(directions)
        for direction in directions:
            if self.env.move_agent(direction):
                return


    def deliberative_behavior(self):
        # Simple goal-oriented strategy
        goal_x, goal_y = self.env.goal
        pos_x, pos_y = self.env.agent_pos


        if goal_x > pos_x and
self.env.move_agent("down"):
            return
        elif goal_x < pos_x and
self.env.move_agent("up"):
            return
```

```python
        elif goal_y > pos_y and
self.env.move_agent("right"):

            return

        elif goal_y < pos_y and
self.env.move_agent("left"):

            return

        else:

            self.reactive_behavior()


    def run(self):

        while not self.env.is_goal_reached():

            self.deliberative_behavior()

            print(f"Agent moved to:
{self.env.agent_pos}")

        print("Goal reached!")
```

Explanation:

- Deliberative Behavior: Moves the agent closer to the goal.
- Reactive Behavior: Randomly moves to avoid obstacles when blocked.

Step 4: Run the Agent

```python
# Initialize the environment

obstacles = [[1, 1], [2, 2], [3, 3]]

goal = [4, 4]
```

```
env = GridWorld(size=5, obstacles=obstacles,
goal=goal)


# Initialize and run the hybrid agent

agent = HybridAgent(env)

agent.run()
```

Expected Output:

Agent moved to: [1, 0]

Agent moved to: [2, 0]

Agent moved to: [3, 0]

Agent moved to: [4, 0]

Agent moved to: [4, 1]

Agent moved to: [4, 2]

Agent moved to: [4, 3]

Agent moved to: [4, 4]

Goal reached!

Real-World Examples of Evolving AI Agents

1. Self-Driving Cars (Tesla, Waymo): Combine reactive behaviors (avoiding obstacles) with deliberative planning (navigating routes).

2. Autonomous Drones: Use adaptive learning to adjust flight paths in response to wind, obstacles, and battery levels.

3. AI Assistants (Alexa, Google Assistant): Integrate proactive features (reminders) with reactive responses (answering queries).

Best Practices for Designing Advanced AI Agents

1. Balance Reactivity and Deliberation: Hybrid agents should combine immediate reactions with thoughtful planning.
2. Use Modular Components: Separate perception, decision-making, and action layers for flexibility.
3. Incorporate Learning: Enable agents to improve over time using feedback and data.
4. Ensure Scalability: Design agents that can scale across systems or environments.
5. Focus on Explainability: Agents should explain decisions to improve user trust and transparency.

10.2 Integrating LangChain and LangGraph with Emerging Technologies

As artificial intelligence continues to evolve, integrating AI frameworks like LangChain and LangGraph with emerging technologies is essential to building smarter, more adaptive, and scalable solutions. Combining these frameworks with cutting-edge tools in cloud computing, blockchain, edge computing, and quantum computing allows developers to design intelligent workflows that are more efficient, secure, and responsive. In this section, we'll explore how LangChain and LangGraph can be integrated with these emerging technologies, provide real-world use cases, and share hands-on code examples to demonstrate practical applications.

1. Integration with Cloud Computing

Cloud computing is central to deploying scalable AI systems. Platforms like AWS, Google Cloud Platform (GCP), and Azure provide on-demand infrastructure to support large-scale AI workflows.

Why Cloud Integration Matters

- Scalability: Automatically scales resources based on workload.
- Cost-Efficiency: Pay-as-you-go models minimize infrastructure costs.
- High Availability: Ensures continuous uptime and disaster recovery.

Example: Deploying LangChain Workflow on AWS Lambda

Objective: Automate a data analysis workflow that scales dynamically using AWS Lambda.

Step 1: Install Dependencies

```
pip install langchain boto3
```

Step 2: Python Script for Lambda Deployment

```
import json

import boto3

from langchain.chains import SimpleChain


# Define a simple data processing workflow
```

```python
def load_data():

    return {"sales": [100, 200, 300], "expenses":
[50, 80, 100]}


def analyze_data(data):

    profit = sum(data["sales"]) -
sum(data["expenses"])

    return {"profit": profit}


# Combine workflow using LangChain

workflow = SimpleChain(steps=[load_data,
analyze_data])


def lambda_handler(event, context):

    result = workflow.run()

    return {

        'statusCode': 200,

        'body': json.dumps(result)

    }
```

Explanation:

- AWS Lambda handles execution without managing servers.
- LangChain automates data loading and analysis.

2. Integration with Edge Computing

Edge computing brings data processing closer to the data source, reducing latency and bandwidth usage. For real-time AI applications, this is a game-changer.

Why Edge Integration Matters

- Low Latency: Critical for real-time decision-making.
- Bandwidth Efficiency: Reduces the need to transfer large datasets to the cloud.
- Offline Operation: Enables devices to work without internet connectivity.

Example: Running LangChain Workflow on Raspberry Pi

Objective: Automate temperature monitoring on a Raspberry Pi to trigger alerts if the temperature exceeds a threshold.

Python Script for Edge Deployment

```python
import random

import time

from langchain.chains import SimpleChain


# Simulate temperature sensor data
def read_temperature():
    return random.uniform(20.0, 40.0)


# Analyze temperature data
```

```
def analyze_temperature(temp):

    if temp > 30:

        return "ALERT: High Temperature!"

    return "Temperature is normal."


# Create the workflow

workflow = SimpleChain(steps=[read_temperature,
analyze_temperature])


# Continuous monitoring

while True:

    result = workflow.run()

    print(result)

    time.sleep(5)   # Check every 5 seconds
```

Explanation:

- Raspberry Pi continuously checks temperature data.
- If the temperature exceeds 30°C, it triggers an alert in real-time.

3. Integration with Blockchain for Secure AI Workflows

Blockchain technology offers secure, transparent, and tamper-proof solutions for recording and verifying AI workflow executions.

Why Blockchain Integration Matters

- Data Integrity: Immutable records of AI decision-making processes.
- Security: Protects against data tampering and unauthorized access.
- Transparency: Provides audit trails for AI actions.

Example: Verifying AI Workflow Results with Ethereum

Objective: Record the output of an AI workflow on the Ethereum blockchain for auditability.

Step 1: Install Web3 Library

```
pip install web3
```

Step 2: Python Script for Blockchain Logging

```
from web3 import Web3

from langchain.chains import SimpleChain


# Connect to Ethereum network (e.g., Infura)

web3 =
Web3(Web3.HTTPProvider('https://mainnet.infura.io
/v3/YOUR_INFURA_PROJECT_ID'))


# Example private key and account

private_key = "YOUR_PRIVATE_KEY"

account =
web3.eth.account.privateKeyToAccount(private_key)
```

```python
# Simple workflow

def load_data():

    return {"sales": 500, "expenses": 300}


def analyze_data(data):

    return f"Profit: {data['sales'] -
data['expenses']}"


workflow = SimpleChain(steps=[load_data,
analyze_data])


# Run the workflow and record on blockchain
def record_on_blockchain():

    result = workflow.run()

    txn = {

        'to': account.address,

        'value': 0,

        'gas': 2000000,

        'gasPrice': web3.toWei('50', 'gwei'),

        'nonce':
web3.eth.getTransactionCount(account.address),
```

```
    'data': web3.toHex(text=result)

}

    signed_txn =
web3.eth.account.signTransaction(txn,
private_key)

    tx_hash =
web3.eth.sendRawTransaction(signed_txn.rawTransac
tion)

    print(f"Workflow result recorded with TXN
hash: {web3.toHex(tx_hash)}")



record_on_blockchain()
```

Explanation:

- After executing the workflow, the result is securely logged on the Ethereum blockchain.
- This ensures transparency and prevents tampering.

4. Integration with Quantum Computing

Quantum computing has the potential to revolutionize AI by solving problems that are computationally intractable for classical computers.

Why Quantum Integration Matters

- Optimization: Solves large-scale optimization problems faster.
- Complex Simulations: Efficiently simulates physical systems.
- Machine Learning: Accelerates complex model training.

Example: Quantum-Powered AI Workflow

Objective: Use quantum algorithms to optimize AI workflow execution.

Step 1: Install Qiskit

```
pip install qiskit
```

Step 2: Python Script for Quantum Optimization

```
from qiskit import Aer, transpile

from qiskit.algorithms import VQE

from qiskit.circuit.library import TwoLocal

from qiskit.primitives import Estimator


# Define a quantum circuit for optimization

qc = TwoLocal(4, ['ry', 'rz'], 'cz', reps=3,
entanglement='full')


# Set up the quantum optimizer

optimizer = VQE(ansatz=qc, estimator=Estimator(),
optimizer='SPSA')


# Run the optimizer

result = optimizer.run()
```

```
print(f"Optimal parameters:
{result.optimal_parameters}")
```

Explanation:

- VQE is used to solve complex optimization problems that could improve AI model performance.
- Future AI workflows could leverage quantum optimization for faster decision-making.

Best Practices for Integration

1. Security First: Encrypt data and follow best practices when integrating with sensitive platforms like blockchain or IoT.
2. Modular Design: Keep integration components modular for easy updates and scalability.
3. Resource Management: Monitor and optimize resource usage in cloud and edge environments.
4. Failover Mechanisms: Implement fallback strategies for cloud, edge, and blockchain integrations.

10.3 Open Source Contributions and Community Involvement

Open-source software is the backbone of modern technology. It fosters innovation, accelerates development, and democratizes access to powerful tools and frameworks. The growth and success of platforms like **LangChain** and **LangGraph** are deeply rooted in the active involvement of open-source communities. These communities bring together developers, researchers, and enthusiasts worldwide to collaboratively solve complex problems, improve functionality, and expand the capabilities of these tools.

Why Open Source Contributions Matter

Open-source contributions are more than just writing code. They involve creating documentation, designing tools, reporting bugs, and fostering collaboration. Here's why open-source contributions are crucial:

1. Accelerates Innovation

- Collective problem-solving leads to faster innovation.
- Diverse contributors bring fresh perspectives and ideas.

Example:
LangChain's rapid adoption and growth have been possible due to community-driven improvements, including connectors for new data sources and integrations with other AI frameworks.

2. Encourages Transparency

- Open access to code allows users to understand, audit, and trust the software.
- Transparency builds trust in AI systems, especially when dealing with sensitive data.

3. Fosters Collaboration

- Contributions bring together people from different backgrounds and skill levels.
- Developers, researchers, and businesses collaborate to solve real-world problems.

4. Provides Learning and Career Opportunities

- Open-source participation enhances coding, design, and problem-solving skills.
- Contributors gain recognition and career advancement opportunities.

Ways to Contribute to LangChain and LangGraph

Contributing to open-source projects like LangChain and LangGraph can take many forms beyond just coding. Here are several ways you can get involved:

1. Code Contributions

If you're a developer, contributing code is the most direct way to help improve these frameworks.

- Fix Bugs: Identify and resolve issues listed in the project's issue tracker.
- Add New Features: Propose and implement new features or tools.
- Improve Performance: Optimize existing workflows and algorithms.

2. Documentation Improvements

Good documentation is as important as good code. Many developers hesitate to use a tool if it lacks clear, concise documentation.

- Write Tutorials and Guides: Help new users understand how to use the tools.
- Clarify Existing Docs: Simplify complex explanations.
- Update for New Features: Ensure the documentation stays current.

3. Report Bugs and Suggest Enhancements

- Bug Reporting: Share detailed bug reports to help maintainers identify and fix issues.
- Feature Requests: Suggest practical features that could benefit users.

4. Community Engagement

- Answer Questions: Help users by answering questions on forums or discussion boards.
- Review Pull Requests: Assist maintainers by reviewing contributions from others.
- Host Workshops: Organize events to teach others how to use or contribute to these tools.

Step-by-Step Guide to Contributing

Here's how you can start contributing to LangChain or LangGraph:

Step 1: Fork and Clone the Repository

```
# Fork the repository on GitHub, then clone it

git clone
https://github.com/your-username/langchain.git

cd langchain
```

Step 2: Set Up the Development Environment

```
# Install dependencies

pip install -r requirements.txt
```

Step 3: Create a New Branch

```
# Always create a new branch for your feature or
fix

git checkout -b feature/new-tool
```

Step 4: Implement Your Changes

Let's say you're adding a new tool for sentiment analysis:

```
from langchain.tools import BaseTool
```

```python
class SentimentAnalysisTool(BaseTool):

    def run(self, text):

        if "bad" in text:

            return "Negative sentiment detected."
        elif "good" in text:

            return "Positive sentiment detected."
        else:

            return "Neutral sentiment."


# Example usage

tool = SentimentAnalysisTool()

print(tool.run("The product is really good!"))
```

Step 5: Test Your Changes

```
# Run tests to ensure nothing breaks

pytest tests/
```

Step 6: Commit and Push Changes

```
git add .

git commit -m "Added SentimentAnalysisTool for
text sentiment detection"

git push origin feature/new-tool
```

Step 7: Submit a Pull Request

- Go to the repository on GitHub.
- Click "New Pull Request".
- Provide a clear description of what you've changed.

Tip: Reference related issues to provide context.

Real-World Examples of Open Source Impact

1. LangChain Community Contributions

LangChain has grown quickly due to valuable community contributions, such as:

- API Integrations: Contributors have built connectors for new APIs, expanding LangChain's versatility.
- Performance Improvements: Developers have optimized workflows, making them faster and more scalable.

2. LangGraph Enhancements

Contributors to LangGraph have:

- Designed Visualization Tools: Tools to visualize complex AI workflows have improved debugging and monitoring.
- Expanded Documentation: Community members have created detailed guides for using LangGraph in production environments.

Best Practices for Open-Source Contribution

1. Start Small and Stay Consistent

Begin with small contributions like fixing typos, updating documentation, or resolving simple bugs. Over time, you can work on more complex features.

2. Follow Contribution Guidelines

Most projects have contribution guidelines in a CONTRIBUTING.md file. Always follow coding standards, commit message formats, and pull request protocols.

3. Communicate Effectively

- Open issues before implementing major changes to get feedback.
- Keep pull requests focused and well-documented.
- Be respectful when discussing changes or reviewing others' work.

4. Test Before You Commit

Always test your changes to ensure they work and don't introduce bugs. If the project has automated tests, run them locally before submitting your work.

5. Engage with the Community

Join discussions on Slack, Discord, or forums related to the project. Collaboration fosters better ideas and solutions.

Exercise: Make Your First Contribution

1. Fork the LangChain repository.
2. Add a Custom Tool (e.g., a weather API integration).
3. Write Documentation for your tool.
4. Submit a Pull Request.

Benefits of Community Involvement

For Individuals

- Skill Development: Gain hands-on experience with real-world projects.

- Networking: Connect with experts and like-minded contributors.
- Portfolio Building: Showcase your work to potential employers.

For Organizations

- Faster Innovation: Leverage collective intelligence for faster problem-solving.
- Community Trust: Open-source involvement builds credibility.
- Custom Solutions: Adapt open-source tools to meet business needs.

Open-source contributions are the driving force behind the rapid growth and improvement of frameworks like LangChain and LangGraph. Whether you're fixing bugs, writing documentation, building tools, or helping others in the community, every contribution adds value. By engaging with open-source communities, you not only help improve the tools you use but also sharpen your skills, expand your network, and make a real impact in the field of AI. Start small, stay consistent, and become part of the innovation that's shaping the future of AI workflows.

10.4 Predictions for the Future of Dynamic AI Systems

Dynamic AI systems are revolutionizing industries by automating complex workflows, making intelligent decisions, and continuously adapting to new information. As we look toward the future, several technological advancements will reshape how dynamic AI systems are designed, deployed, and scaled. This section will explore well-grounded predictions for the evolution of dynamic AI systems, supported by real-world examples and practical insights.

1. AI Systems Will Become Fully Autonomous

Prediction

Dynamic AI systems will transition from being task-specific to becoming fully autonomous entities capable of self-management, self-learning, and self-repair. This evolution will minimize human intervention, allowing AI systems to identify problems, make decisions, and optimize their workflows without needing constant oversight.

Key Features

- Autonomous Decision-Making: AI agents will independently make high-stakes decisions.
- Self-Optimization: Systems will identify inefficiencies and reconfigure workflows.
- Adaptive Learning: Continuous learning from real-time data will refine AI models.

Real-World Example

Autonomous Supply Chains:
Future supply chain management systems will autonomously manage inventory, optimize logistics, and resolve disruptions in real time. For example, a supply chain AI might reroute deliveries automatically if it detects a weather-related delay.

Code Illustration: Self-Optimizing Workflow

```python
from langchain.chains import SimpleChain

import random



# Simulated task performance metrics
```

```python
def measure_performance():

    return random.uniform(0.5, 1.0)  # Simulated
efficiency score


# Dynamic optimization step

def optimize_workflow(score):

    if score < 0.7:

        return "Adjust workflow parameters for
better performance."

    return "Workflow running optimally."


# Combine into a dynamic workflow

workflow =
SimpleChain(steps=[measure_performance,
optimize_workflow])


# Run the adaptive workflow

result = workflow.run()

print(result)
```

Explanation:
This workflow simulates performance monitoring and adjusts its operation automatically when performance drops.

2. Multi-Agent Collaboration Will Dominate Complex Systems

Prediction

AI systems will evolve into ecosystems of multi-agent systems (MAS) where specialized agents collaborate to solve large-scale problems. These agents will communicate, negotiate, and dynamically delegate tasks to optimize outcomes.

Key Features

- Distributed Intelligence: Multiple agents work concurrently on sub-tasks.
- Negotiation and Coordination: Agents will negotiate resources and priorities.
- Goal-Oriented Behavior: Agents will align tasks with overarching goals.

Real-World Example

Smart Cities:

In future smart cities, multi-agent systems will manage traffic, energy grids, and public safety in real time. Traffic signals, public transit, and emergency services will collaborate autonomously to reduce congestion and improve response times.

Code Illustration: Multi-Agent Collaboration

```python
import threading

import time


class Agent(threading.Thread):

    def __init__(self, name, task):

        threading.Thread.__init__(self)
```

```python
        self.name = name

        self.task = task


    def run(self):

        print(f"{self.name} started
{self.task}.")

        time.sleep(2)   # Simulate task duration

        print(f"{self.name} completed
{self.task}.")


# Create agents with different tasks
agents = [

    Agent("Agent-1", "Data Processing"),

    Agent("Agent-2", "Model Training"),

    Agent("Agent-3", "Real-Time Monitoring")

]


# Start all agents
for agent in agents:

    agent.start()
```

```
# Wait for all agents to complete

for agent in agents:

    agent.join()


print("All tasks completed.")
```

Each agent works on a different task simultaneously, demonstrating distributed task execution.

3. AI Systems Will Prioritize Ethical and Transparent Decision-Making

Prediction

As AI systems become more autonomous, ethical AI and explainability will become foundational requirements. AI systems will need to justify their decisions in ways that are understandable and auditable by humans.

Key Features

- Explainable AI (XAI): Clear explanations for decisions.
- Fairness and Bias Mitigation: Built-in safeguards against bias.
- Compliance: Automatic adherence to ethical and legal frameworks.

Real-World Example

Healthcare Diagnostics:
AI diagnostic systems will not only suggest treatments but explain why a specific treatment is recommended. This transparency is crucial for patient trust and medical accountability.

Code Illustration: Explainable Decision-Making

```
def medical_diagnosis(symptoms):

    if "fever" in symptoms and "cough" in
symptoms:

        return "Diagnosis: Flu", "Reason:
Detected symptoms of fever and cough."

    return "Diagnosis: Unknown", "Reason:
Symptoms do not match known patterns."



# Simulate diagnosis

diagnosis, explanation =
medical_diagnosis(["fever", "cough"])

print(diagnosis)

print(explanation)
```

The AI not only gives a diagnosis but also explains the reasoning, promoting transparency.

4. Real-Time Adaptive Learning Will Become Standard

Prediction

AI systems will no longer rely solely on pre-trained models. Instead, they will adapt and learn continuously from real-time data, allowing them to stay relevant in rapidly changing environments.

Key Features

- Online Learning: Models update in real-time as new data arrives.
- Context Awareness: Immediate adaptation to environmental changes.
- Continuous Improvement: Models evolve without retraining from scratch.

Real-World Example

Financial Fraud Detection:
Fraud detection systems will continuously learn from new fraudulent patterns, adapting their detection strategies in real time to counter evolving tactics.

Code Illustration: Online Learning Simulation

```python
from sklearn.linear_model import SGDClassifier

import numpy as np


# Simulate streaming data

X_stream = np.random.rand(100, 5)

y_stream = np.random.choice([0, 1], 100)


# Initialize online learning model

model = SGDClassifier(loss='log_loss')


# Simulate real-time learning

for i in range(0, 100, 10):
```

```
    X_batch, y_batch = X_stream[i:i+10],
y_stream[i:i+10]

    model.partial_fit(X_batch, y_batch,
classes=[0, 1])

    print(f"Batch {i//10 + 1} trained.")
```

This model continuously updates with new data batches, adapting in real time.

5. Seamless Integration Across Technologies

Prediction

Dynamic AI systems will integrate seamlessly across various technologies, including IoT, blockchain, and quantum computing, enabling cross-platform intelligence.

Key Features

- Interoperability: Connects effortlessly with diverse technologies.
- Decentralization: Blockchain secures AI workflows.
- Enhanced Processing: Quantum computing accelerates complex computations.

Real-World Example

Autonomous Vehicles:
Future autonomous vehicles will combine IoT for real-time data, AI for decision-making, and blockchain for secure data sharing.

Code Illustration: IoT Integration with LangChain

```
from langchain.chains import SimpleChain
```

```python
def read_sensor():

    return {"speed": 60, "obstacle_distance": 10}


def control_vehicle(data):

    if data["obstacle_distance"] < 15:

        return "Apply brakes."

    return "Maintain speed."


# Workflow combining sensor data and
decision-making

vehicle_workflow =
SimpleChain(steps=[read_sensor, control_vehicle])

print(vehicle_workflow.run())
```

This workflow uses IoT sensor data to make real-time driving decisions.

These advancements will redefine industries, elevate user experiences, and open doors to innovation on an unprecedented scale. Developers and organizations that embrace these trends will be well-equipped to lead in this new era of intelligent, dynamic systems.

Conclusion

Throughout this book, *Agent Flow: Designing Dynamic AI Workflows with LangChain and LangGraph*, we have explored the foundational concepts, practical applications, and advanced techniques required to design, build, and deploy dynamic AI systems. The journey began with understanding the importance of AI workflows and progressed through building intelligent agents, integrating external tools, managing complex workflows, and deploying scalable solutions in real-world scenarios.

At the core of this exploration are two groundbreaking frameworks—LangChain and LangGraph. These tools empower developers to move beyond traditional static AI models, enabling the creation of adaptive, scalable, and autonomous systems. They provide the building blocks to design workflows that are intelligent, flexible, and capable of handling real-world complexity.

Key Points

Let's revisit the most important lessons and skills gained throughout this book:

1. Understanding Dynamic AI Workflows: You learned how dynamic workflows differ from static processes by adapting to changing inputs and conditions in real-time.

2. Building Intelligent Agents: We explored various agent architectures—reactive, proactive, and hybrid—and how to implement them effectively for complex tasks.

3. Mastering LangChain and LangGraph: You gained hands-on experience with these frameworks, understanding how to build chains, create adaptive workflows, and manage

states and transitions.

4. Integration with External Tools and APIs: You discovered how to extend AI capabilities by integrating third-party APIs, custom tools, and specialized data sources.

5. Error Handling and Workflow Recovery: We covered strategies for making workflows more resilient through proactive error handling and recovery mechanisms.

6. Scalability and Deployment: You learned how to deploy AI systems in production environments, ensuring they are secure, scalable, and optimized for performance.

7. Ethical AI and Security: The book emphasized the importance of designing AI systems that are ethical, transparent, and secure.

8. Open Source and Community Involvement: We highlighted how contributing to and engaging with the open-source community can drive innovation and enhance your professional growth.

9. Future Trends in AI Systems: Finally, we explored emerging trends shaping the future of dynamic AI, such as autonomous agents, multi-agent collaboration, explainable AI, and integration with cutting-edge technologies like blockchain, IoT, and quantum computing.

Artificial intelligence is a rapidly evolving field. The concepts, tools, and best practices covered in this book represent the current state-of-the-art, but the journey doesn't end here. As technologies advance and new challenges emerge, the need for dynamic, adaptive AI workflows will only grow.

The next generation of AI systems will be more autonomous, collaborative, and integrated across diverse technologies. Staying ahead in this evolving landscape requires continuous learning, experimentation, and innovation.

Practical Next Steps

Here's how you can continue your journey:

- Apply What You've Learned: Start integrating LangChain and LangGraph into your projects. Experiment with real-world data, external APIs, and multi-agent systems.
- Contribute to Open Source: Join the communities behind LangChain, LangGraph, and related projects. Share your ideas, contribute code, and collaborate with others.
- Stay Current: Follow industry news, research papers, and updates to stay informed about the latest advancements in AI workflows and intelligent agents.
- Explore Emerging Technologies: Deepen your understanding of edge computing, quantum computing, blockchain, and how they intersect with AI workflows.
- Focus on Ethical AI: Prioritize transparency, fairness, and security in your designs. Responsible AI is not just a best practice—it's a necessity.

The field of artificial intelligence holds incredible promise, and dynamic AI workflows are at the heart of this transformation. By combining intelligence, adaptability, and scalability, these systems are shaping industries and redefining how we interact with technology.

Building intelligent, dynamic workflows is more than just implementing the latest tools—it's about solving real-world problems in meaningful ways. Whether you're automating business processes, enhancing customer experiences, or developing new AI-driven products, the knowledge you've gained equips you to create solutions that are not only functional but also innovative and impactful.

The future belongs to those who are ready to build, adapt, and innovate. You now have the knowledge and tools to be part of this future.

Now it's your turn. Let's create the future of dynamic AI.

James Acklin

www.ingramcontent.com/pod-product-compliance
Lightning Source LLC
LaVergne TN
LVHW081511050326
832903LV00025B/1451